# FOOT PRINTS OF ETERNITY

*Ancient Wisdom Applied to Modern Psychology*

*By Robert D. Waterman, EdD, LPCC*

Copyright © 2006 by Robert D. Waterman

ISBN  0-7414-3115-7

*Robert D. Waterman*
*41 Verano Loop*
*Santa Fe, NM 87508*
*505-466-8385*
*rdw2110@aol.com*
*http://mystery-school.com*

*Published by:*

PUBLISHING.COM

*1094 New DeHaven Street, Suite 100*
*West Conshohocken, PA 19428-2713*
*Info@buybooksontheweb.com*
*www.buybooksontheweb.com*
*Toll-free  (877) BUY BOOK*
*Local Phone (610) 941-9999*
*Fax  (610) 941-9959*

Printed in the United States of America

Printed on Recycled Paper

Published  April 2006

## APPRECIATION

Teachers are essential. They challenge
false perceptions and show the way
to higher consciousness,
passed the illusion of the
lower worlds. Thank you to:
John-Roger,
Neva Dell Hunter,
Ellavivian Power,
and my students,
who show me the many ways
that God expresses itself, and
my wife, whose love
is a continual reflection
that promotes clarity and grace,
making God our Home.

## DEDICATION

To the transformation
of the human condition
through the enlightenment
of individuals.

# FOOT PRINTS

We are woven together into a whole.
Somewhat unconscious at first, we move along the face of eternity
looking for an image of ourselves,
to know ourselves.
A foot print.

What motivates us?
How does the universe enfold itself into an individual?
How does holiness unfold itself into human form?
We look inward through the undulating patterns of light
and sound and outward into the reflection of self in the multiform
drama of life.
We are a deep mystery.

Illumination only deepens the mystery.
Enlightenment gives us truth, but no language.
For lack of a language by which we can articulate the encrypted
nuances of the fabric of self, we simply claim that we walk
this earth as *holiness,*
finding its way home.

At first, we want to know why we suffer.
Then, we realize that suffering is our way of realizing that there is
more to our humanity than this painful smallness.
In a sense, it is God's fault.
We will not rest until we actualize the God-quality within us.

The quest for wealth, power, safety, and security
are temporary distractions from self.
They do not satisfy the need to love and be loved.
They do not solve the fear.
Only love answers all,
awakening the sleeping places,
the remembrance of home.

The lurking shadows are not demons or enemies.
They are emissaries of our forgotten virtues and noble selves
seeking their creator:
seeking wholeness, union, promises of the One.

Love is the source of all truth.
Truth reveals itself through the ruthless surrender to love.
We must be fearless.

Our great deeds do no make us great or safe.
They reveal.
They are testament to an innate truth.
Claiming our greatness is not fame.
Fame is the reminder.
It is an image on a mirror:
a reflection.
Look through the glass,
through the darkness,
face to face.
Truth.

Not the truth that struts in our righteous postures,
and addictions to our fine thoughts.
Rather,
the truth that weaves itself through our tragedies and triumphs,
that whispers to us in the soft folds of our heart.

When all is said and done,
we will reflect upon our sojourn, and say:
"Eternity walked here."

# TABLE OF CONTENTS

# INTRODUCTION

Psychology is at a crossroads. Behind the scenes, empirical and heuristic approaches to the science of psychology collaborate with mysticism and quantum physics to find a new technology and vocabulary of consciousness. Meanwhile, institutionalized psychology defends its arbitrary claim to exclusive wisdom, as it struggles to remain the "academy" in spite of the ever-increasing use of drugs to ameliorate symptoms, the continued fragmentation of society, and the gradual unraveling of its emotional and mental fabric. Even religion confronts itself with its own dogmatism, hoping to find grace through its self elevated view of its own righteousness. Yet others, from all perspectives, turn inward, there to find an awaiting covenant with eternity.

Currently, each school of psychology has its own province. For example: *Behaviorism* changes our behavior. *Psychodynamics* assists us to integrate and reorganize our healthy ego structure. *Humanism* processes our emotions and connects our actions with our feelings in a way that is congruent with our heart. *Archetypal* makes conscious our unconscious drives and facilitates actualization and fulfillment. *Transpersonal* connects us to our transcendental self, and awakens our awareness to universal themes and enlightenment. Viewing these various approaches as separate only perpetuates the perennial turf war of academic prestige and power, as it has for centuries. Taken together, however, they form a coherent model of the multidimensional human and its natural quest for health. Yet, we continue to divide up the human, perpetuating the universal dysfunction.

As an undergraduate, I began to see that fear was the glue of professional education and practice. Fear driven professionalism instills a subliminal adversarial tension into our enquiry and dialogue. Trust in ourselves and our inherent ability to know opens our ability to know directly from our experience. Thus, my heroes became the theorists and teachers who used first-hand phenomenology as their research methodology. Carl Jung, Fritze Perls, Carl Rogers, Abraham Maslow, and Rollo May were griping examples from the psychological perspective, as were David Bohm and Edmund Husserl from the scientific perspectives. I found the work of spiritual travelers to be equally exciting, as represented by Hermes Trismesgistus, Pythagoras, Lao Tzu, Rumi, Gautama Buddha, Jesus Christ, Ralph Waldo Emerson,

Phineus Parkhurst Quimby, and Rudolph Steiner. All of these individuals trusted who they were and used that center to discover truth.

Other forces were at play for me as well. On the eve of the 60's, as a participant in a sensory deprivation experiment, I discovered that spiritual realities were directly observable. In the mid-60's, as a participant in the civil rights movement, I discovered that character strength could be a force for social transformation. Meanwhile, Quantum Physics gave birth to the notion of the "observer effect"– that observation itself affects outcome. Gone was the illusion of certainty. I discovered that there is no "objective" science or objective God. I loved the way the 60's challenged my 50's reality. The social order appeared ready to deconstruct itself and to open to a new spirit of human potential. My academic goal thus became one of blending material and metaphysical wisdom into a unified curriculum for the purpose of individual well being and social change.

The journey toward that goal resulted in the founding and accreditation of Southwestern College in Santa Fe, New Mexico, as a graduate school for Counseling Psychology and Art Therapy with a core curriculum that integrated conventional and spiritual wisdom within an academic framework. The core curriculum focused on character first, then professional orientation. It was a "cleansing of the heart" first approach. This was, to me, an antidote to the conventional "washing of the brain" method used in most professional education.

My intention in this writing is to incite a discussion and open a doorway in the awareness of academic psychology and counselor education through which the force of spirit and soul can flow into our minds, open our hearts, and elevate our consciousness. If we are to discover the secrets of life, we need courage and trust in our capacity to know. Those secrets *are* available to us. The idea that the ancients were enlightened is more than just a mythology. By ancient, I do not mean primitive. Primitives share with moderns the amnesia of the original soul. Ancient wisdom is indigenous and transcendental. Indigenous wisdom tells us where we are, and remembers the *soul of the earth*, pulling access through her from the great heart of the universe. Transcendental wisdom opens a path inward, accessing the celestial vortex of light and sound that returns us *home*. When we know our true source and place, we have the key to transforming life on earth into grace.

Paradoxically, we are evolving to remember our intentional

design. Myths point to prior high points in human evolution that have all but disappeared into the sands of time. Yet their meanings now re-awaken in the contours of our hearts. In our quantum reality, the past exists as a dimension of the present. When we are unconscious of this, the errors of the past continue to shape the present. When we are conscious of it, the ancient wisdom of the soul permeates our contemporary awareness, and we make life new.

This writing is an invitation to loosen your perception, allowing your mind to reach out to new thoughts and your intelligence to ascend to new levels of your heart. Once that occurs, your reflection on the material will open internally to the wisdom of the soul. From that opening will come the knowledge of our complete nature and our role in eternity. Our clients, students, colleagues, and friends will be the beneficiaries.

You may need to be read some passages slowly, allowing time for your reflection. Listen deeply. The inner commentary of your intuition will more often be the point. I recommend that you skip parts that seem unresponsive and take the book as a whole, returning to seemingly obscure portions after you have tried some of the experiential exercises. As you explore the experiential exercises, the intellectual aspects of the text will make more sense to you. In any case: enjoy. Joy is always a key.

## Chapter One

# TRANSCENDENTAL PHENOMENOLOGY

The physical body is an epicenter of experience. Our bodies are the densest membrane of our soul. At first, our bodies do not appear to be a *surface*, like that of a ball, or a planet. Our skin seems like one, but the entire body? Consider that each organ, cell, fiber, even DNA, is actually a dimensional surface, contoured and folded over and into itself. We see the surface, but not the morphogenic field that lives in 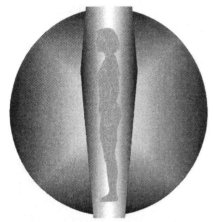 and around the surface. From the perspective of the morphogenic field, visible surfaces are merely the "tip of the iceberg." Appearances in the physical world unfold from the multidimensional matrix-fields in which they are nested. When we consider these physics of the "self," we introduce our minds to a new way of thinking. By practicing such *quantum thinking,* we become conscious explorers of life through the process of inner experience, discovering the covenant of the soul. No matter how far we journey, the way home is always accessible, coded into our essence. We are driven to actualize our holiness in physical form, then transcend that manifestation and return home. This is the agreement that guides us. The "father of quantum physics," David Bohm, saw life as an unfolding and infolding holomovement of nested realities. Our experience of continuity occurs from the on/off pulsing of a whole that is continually coordinating all with all. The spiritual journey is the continuity of the soul. The ego-mind believes that we are the belief structure of our self-concept and strives to preserve our sense of continuity by defending the status-quo self. Here we have a key perspective on the structure of experience. The soul/ego dynamic is the tension from which all psychological adventures are both formed and transformed.

Like the macrocosm, the body exists in a sphere of energy. The sphere is bounded by a surface and contains our personal sentience. According to ancient teachings, this sphere – a full two arms reach in diameter around our body – is also informed by the contours of sacred geometry. All the dynamics of our personal experience of self are revealed within it. This space, and these forms, organize our perception, our interface with life. This interface, the "shape" and character of the surface where we meet the world, affects not only how we see, but how we in turn are "seen" by life. It determines the holographic shape that life takes on around us as it unfolds to us as "reality." Our sentience extends beyond our personal sphere into cultural, collective, archetypal and universal spheres. At each level of awakening and access, our perceived reality changes. Thus life, as a single unifying organism, responds to the invitation of our perception. In the research and therapeutic style of phenomenology, when we deconstruct our false beliefs, life automatically presents truth. In other words, perception is the means by which we select our relationship to the macrocosm and also how the macrocosm "selects" its appearance to us. The universe meets us at the epicenter of our attention.

Our lives, as journeys of attention, provide a context for the soul to evolve through relationship. One of relationship's most potent forms is the ongoing dialectic between *thing* and *no-thing*. "Thing" is form, fact, material, or sedimented beliefs. "Thing," in this sense, is also called *noema*. "No-thing" is essence, intentionality, soul, spirit, and truth – also known as *noesis*. We develop our humanity by participating in this noema/noesis dialectic, becoming aware of it in ourselves and in our lives. We live in this *noetic* reality for the purpose of fulfilling life, as life knows itself through each of us.

When distracted by fear, our center goes dark and love becomes an external phantom that promises everything, but continually eludes our grasp. Our virtue is held externally captive by our perception. Yet fears and sedimented beliefs – *noema* – provide a doorway into transcendental illumination. When we come into the moment, into intimacy with *noesis*, we experience the truth behind our beliefs and fears. All our elements are then working in concert, and we experience ourselves as a pulsating force field of love that unfolds from the essence of life. Our sense of virtue returns to center and is liberated by our perception. Noesis is a *return to soul*.

# EDMUND HUSSERL

In his search for a "science of philosophy," Edmund Husserl became the father of phenomenology. He was interested in developing a systematic protocol for inner discovery, a science of philosophy. In doing so, he re-discovered an ancient wisdom, that perception is the holograph of reality. In phenomenology, the structure of experience is seen as noetic, where creation actualizes purpose, or intention, through the relationship between the noema and noesis. It is how life resolves itself through living. Life, as the field of energy in which we move, is also the context in which the reflexive activity of noema and noesis can create understanding. Noema is the life-hologram that reflects our current reality back to us. In sedimentation especially, it also reflects the conflict between essence and form that has been with us so long that we believe it to be the very nature of our humanity. *"Noegenesis"* occurs when noesis is liberated from sedimented noema. Noegenesis means to apprehend new understanding directly from the experience . The epiphany of *noegenesis,* the experience of *noesis,* is the goal and motivation of Husserl's transcendental phenomenology. It is a science of understanding, in contrast to explanation.

In Husserl's view, that which becomes static dies. Any static thought or thing dies as a means of renewal by returning to its source. A static belief, or thing, can only survive by using energy that is drawn from its surroundings or that is stored within itself. It must then deconstruct, much like the process of fire or decomposition releasing the stored sunlight in wood. We too draw our energy from the field of the universe around us. When we deconstruct a limiting belief, we free its stored energy. So too, when we die we fold our essence back into the *implicate reality.* Without essence to sustain it, the body then deconstructs, yielding back to the universe the residue of our journey here. Dying completes a circle. We return to "no-thing," renewing ourselves for another journey. In noesis, we access living energy. Through noesis, we source the energy for transformation.

There are social dimensions to this process as well. Energy is needed to prolong the viability of any static belief or thing, including cultures or political and religious systems. Consequently, if an "entity" cannot source its own energy, it must take it from a stored source, or from individuals who are able to source their own energy. This need to gain resources by dominating the environment and people is what drives the politics and psychology of fear. It is the force through which all trauma originates, and all wars proceed.

## Phenomenological Reduction

Husserl used the term *reduction* to describe a protocol for deconstructing the fixed, sedimented beliefs that control and shape our perception. In alchemy, this is the process of sedimentation called *calcination*. The term reduction means "purification," and does not imply materialistic "narrowing" or "limiting,"but rather a refining process. It is like the reduction process of purifying metal ore by heating. The aim of reduction is to identify and to deconstruct the clouding limitations and distortions in our perceptual lens that are caused by our sedimented beliefs. While it's true that "seeing is believing," we must first contend with the reality that "believing is seeing," for it is by this mechanism that the external world is subject to our beliefs.

Once our beliefs are formed, we tenaciously and habitually act on those beliefs as if they were sacrosanct truth. As each belief drops into our unconscious mind, it begins to select the reality that we see and the next belief that we accept. This tendency runs far deeper than we generally understand.

Husserl discovered that when he focused on an object while excluding all else, (a process he called "bracketing") and deconstructed the beliefs that were attached to that object, he experienced a perceptual shift that transported him into a state of consciousness in which he could directly comprehend the essence or intentionality (noesis) that formed that object (noema). He called his "science of philosophy:" *transcendental phenomenology,* because his ego moved into a transcendent state of knowing when sufficient deconstruction occurred. Freed of the restriction of sedimented beliefs, his sense of self and reality changed to knowing, rather than belief.

When the grip of fixed beliefs is loosened, our perception changes, freeing the flow of spirit. Within the free movement of spirit,

| TRUTH | FACT |
|-------|------|
| SOUL | EGO |
| ESSENCE | FORM |
| KNOWING | BELIEF |
| NOESIS | NOEMA |

*Through the experiential correlation, we become aware of a two-tracked reality in which soul intends material form and form reflects spiritual intention.*

we know "truth." In the experience of truth through the transcendental mind – the noesis, within "bracketed" noema — Husserl discovered that facts, rather than adding up to truth, are merely *correlated* with, or indexed to, truth. The correlation exists because fact arises from truth and truth intends, or informs, fact. Events, physical forms, and mental constructs – including beliefs – correlate with the a priori intention, or essence, that structured them in the first place. "God created the Heavens and the Earth and saw that it was good." Variation in one corresponds with variation in the other. We gain understanding of this relationship, and our own relationship to it, through *experiential thinking,* by consciously bridging the worlds of essence and form. We thereby also gain the possibility of consciously creating changes in one realm that then create correlated changes in the other.

## The Experience of Noesis

Phenomenology and noetics may seem at first to be very subjective. However, when we take the necessary care to train ourselves in its protocols, we have the bases for a spiritual psychology grounded in scientific protocols that are repeatable and internally consistent. To do this, one's own consciousness must become a research instrument. To be clear, I am expanding the bases of Husserl's science of philosophy into a science of noetics. My intention is to establish a discussion for a legitimate *spiritual physics.* By this, I mean that we can learn to demonstrate the causal, co-creative interaction between consciousness (noesis) and physical reality (noema). As a first step in this process, we must develop ways to test our internal reliability. One way to confirm reliability occurs when several people using the same protocol develop similar conclusions. Another is to produce sufficient like examples until the case is made. Phenomenolgy is a protocol which loosens perceptually fixed realities until it yields the experience of truth, or understanding. The following are two examples in which my experience resulted in a demonstration of spontaneous knowing, as examples of Husserl's phenomenology.

First, I discovered that when I simply focused my attention on the subject of my research, and suspended any thought, belief or interpretation, insights flowed into my awareness, seemingly from an immense depth within me. Sometimes, my awareness transported itself into mind and soul realities. Other times, when I turned my vision inward and focused on the perceptual darkness, a subtle light and archetypal images appeared. I was intuitively teaching myself how to meditate. When I drew and journaled about these images, further insights occurred. There was a call within me to ask for a greater truth, to reach out within myself, forming a greater connection to holiness. I dared to "put away" the security of familiar and accredited things and thoughts, and to touch the void. Life met me there. Waiting right there on the periphery of my attention, life, noesis, spirit, and holiness touched back.

By changing my relationship to the content of my life, I transformed the context of my life. The separation between the physical and metaphysical patterns of life became less distinct to me. Fact and truth were no longer synonymous, yet they continued to be correlated in a way that allowed life to remain coherent to my senses. I found that truth promotes facts and facts reflect truth, yet they are not synonymous.

The second experience was just after army basic training, when I was selected as a subject in a sensory deprivation experiment that the University of Maryland was conducting at the Presidio of Monterey. I was confined to a small room for three days and nights. To limit sensory input, the room was totally dark, sound proof, and kept at body temperature. After about a day or so, the room perceptually lit up. I saw amazing colors, and light radiating from shapes that appeared to float in space. I also had out-of-body experiences in which I flew over the Southern California landscape. All this was unprecedented in my previous experience. Something new lived within me. It shifted my awareness, and I found that even after the experiment was over I was able to sense my relationship with life and with holiness in entirely new ways. The sensory deprivation had deconstructed my mental sedimentation. When the sedimentation is loosened in this way, the experience of noesis naturally emerges. For me, the "safe room" of noema increasingly gave way to noesis, revealing the mystery of worlds beyond. I had stepped into the fourth and fifth dimensions of life as implicate realities of my three dimensional physical life. (As a foot note, the army apparently conducted similar research with hallucinogens. Drugs were not used in this research.)

The sensory deprivation, letting go into it, and paying attention to what happened were all forms of reduction, which together freed my perceptual fixity and enabled me to move into the experience of essence. The resulting change in my perception corresponded to a shift in my center from material mind to spiritual mind. I realized that my conversion and many of the mystical experiences described in the Bible followed a similar protocol. Paul on the road to Damascus, and John

10

on the Isle of Patmos, had also experienced a deconstruction of their perceptual fixity and were transported, as I had been, into a state of consciousness shaped by essence. Milerepa, a renowned Tibetan mystic, described his experience of spending long periods in the limited sensory environment of mountain caves in order to deconstruct his karma and attain enlightenment. Jesus had a similar experience fasting in the wilderness. My own experience of reduction gave me a taste of the accomplishments of these great mystics and demonstrated to me the extreme therapeutic value of these universal techniques. From this understanding, I began to form the theories and practices of Noetic Field Therapy™ (see *Through Eyes of Soul: The Theory and Practice of Noetic Field Therapy*). The keys to this therapy are in understanding the self as energy, the environmental energy field, the nature of perception, the intentional nature of Soul, and the dimensional resource of the noetic field.

## QUANTUM REALITY

"In my house there are many mansions." Physical reality appears to be composed of solids and spaces. In David Bohm's quantum model, the reality results from levels of reality composed of implicate and explicate orders, in which these "solids" exist only as oscillating, flashing on and off, probability fields of dimensional substance. The metaphysical premise "as above, so below" invites us to see the inner and outer, or physical and transcendental worlds, as a causally reflexive relationship. Similarly, Jesus said to Peter: "What you loose on earth, is loosed in heaven, and what you loose in heaven is loosed on earth." David Bohm, in his cosmology of quantum physics, described this enfolding/unfolding relationship as "local events" and "non-local causality," thus, Husserl's noema and noesis.

According to Bohm's view of quantum physics, the physical world, as we know it, contains and is contained in an implicate ordered reality, which is itself contained in an even deeper reality. Each level is transcendent to those within it. In Bohm's words:

*This...is not to be understood solely in terms of a regular arrangement of objects...or as a regular arrangement of events. Rather a total order is contained, in some implicit sense, in each region of space and time. Now, the word 'implicit' is based on the verb 'to implicate.' This means 'to fold inward' (as*

11

*multiplication means 'folding many times').* So we may be led
to explore the notion that in some sense each region contains a
total structure 'enfolded' within it. (Bohm, p. 149).

He describes the broader iteration of this concept when he
states:

*'All implicates all,' even to the extent that 'we ourselves' are
implicated together with 'All that we see and think about.' So
we are present everywhere and at all times, though only
implicately (that is, implicitly). It is only in certain special
orders of description that such objects appear as explicate. The
general law, i.e., holonomy, has to be expressed in all orders, in
which all objects and all times are 'folded together.' (Bohm, p.
167).*

In noetic terms, our multidimensional self implicates our body;
the metaphysical implicates the physical. The implicate, or non-local
order in Bohm's model, is noesis, and the explicate, or local order
(effect), is noema. In both, the impression of linear continuous
appearance gives way to a series of independent events in which each
merely closely resembles the previous moment. In this sense, noesis
unfolds noema and noema enfolds into noesis. In terms of personal
dynamics, I call this pattern of relationships the *noetic field.* The
noetic field is the medium through which the *physics of perception*
cause reality to appear as it does.

From a noetic perspective, it is through consciousness that we
organize and exercise our relationship to the greater consciousness in
which we are contained. The relationship of noesis and noema form
reality as we know it. Perception is our *lens of consciousness,* whether
we are looking into spiritual or physical worlds. Through the protocol
of reduction, we are able to shift our view of reality from the explicate
order of noema to the implicate order of noesis. This is not an
abstraction. It is an experiential shift that has consequence in the
physics of reality formation.

The most direct way to explore the noetic field is by our
experience of it. By exploring the *noetic* field, we find that the very
fabric of life is intelligence. It is spiritual mind, the experience of
which changes with our movement through its domain, as we transport
ourselves into greater and greater implicate realities. The master
intelligence and formative force of the noetic field is universal love. In

12

the quantum sense love and intelligence are aspects of the same consciousness. Conventional science functions as if intelligence stands alone, thus excluding love, as an intentional variable, as the "mother" of intelligence. Intelligence applied without love, fosters conclusions that function inharmoniously with the whole. When we are in the universal mind, we are also in the universal heart. In this sense, as a microcosm, we realize and identify ourselves as pure love. By *pure* love, I mean love that is not attached to belief of any kind, love that is distilled from the deconstruction of our constellated beliefs about love. Love is our passport into these implicate worlds. *Through soul-eyes we can see eternity face to face.*

### The Noetic Microcosm

In the personal realm, or *microcosmically*, our noetic field is the space in which we appear to exist. It is composed of spiritual and archetypal forms, as well as mental, emotional and imaginal structures. It contains our subtle physical body, including the chakras and spiritual glands, as well as our familiar physical body. Again, Bohm provides an apt metaphor:

> *We have seen that in the 'quantum' context, the order of every immediately perceptible aspect of the world is to be regarded as coming out of a more comprehensive implicate order, in which all aspects ultimately merge in the undefinable and immeasurable holomovement... any form of relative autonomy (and heteronomy) is ultimately limited by holonomy, so that in a broad enough context such forms are seen to be merely aspects, relevated in the holomovement, rather than disjoint and separately existent things in interaction. (Bohm, pp. 156-157).*

The noema, thing or belief, is only apparently autonomous. All cause is *non*-local ("local" meaning in the physical dimension) while soul, spirit, or noesis is implicate truth, or causal intentionality. Just *grasping that concept* begins to loosen our perceptual dependence on belief and on an apparently solid physical world. We begin to see and to feel that our only limitation is holonomy – which is everywhere – and that noema, form, thing, belief, ego, and fact are held within that "everywhere" at only apparent locations. Magical!

The term *noetic field* refers to an infinite set of relationships and contexts, all of which exists in a dynamic process of life. In the pre-Nicean (or Gnostic) Lord's prayer, this concept was expressed eloquently as: "The All Parent that is in us and all around us." As we pursue our understanding and mastery of the ancient teachings, we will inevitably transform the structure of our minds. Soul-centered mind and ego-centered mind perceive contrasting realities.

The ego organizes self-awareness around beliefs that are referenced to the physical body and world. We are accustomed to thinking that is based on adversarial methods of discovery. The soul-centered mind thinks in holomovements, so that beliefs and self-concepts are transitional elements of discovery and understanding, yet, ultimately always refers back to soul or center. As such, perception is organized around a central sense of self, and the accustomed ego or material mind serves as an interfacing intelligence, a means of communication between three dimensional thought and noetic consciousness. The noetic or spiritual mind implicates the ego mind, containing its viewpoint and function without being bound by it. Our personal field, in turn, limits our access to those greater fields. However, even though our beliefs limit us, inclusion of a heart energy, such as kindness, keeps us responding to the whole. We have a "physics" of separation and a "physics" of inclusion. Kindness selects the physics of inclusion.

In Bohm's model of the "enfolded universe," a distinction such as an object on the physical level, or a belief on the metaphysical level, is merely a localized phenomenon, or quantum, of the non-localized universal field. What we perceive as localized phenomena are actually just artifacts of the unfolding implicate order. The implicate order is, ultimately, the universal noetic field. Our mastery of this relationship comes through our capacity to experientially contain the correlation between the implicate and explicate orders. We have the inherent capability to navigate the enfolding/unfolding dialectic of the implicate/explicate form of beliefs, and perhaps even of objects. To do so, our focus needs to be on our *relationship* to objects and "objective" realities, and on the correlation of our specific beliefs to the implicating intentions of soul and archetypal formations.

In our daily lives, we form beliefs and enfold them into the unconscious mind. The unconscious mind, in turn, is implicated as an order within our noetic field. And we, as a noetic field of energy, are implicated within a universal noetic field.

As beliefs become sedimented, they bond with objects and circumstances in our perceptual field. Through this process, we create and hold the shape of "our world." Our beliefs behave like fractal equations: reiterating their forms at every component level. As we form our belief systems, we shape our noetic field as a spatial energy form that is unfolding as a localized expression of the implicate universal field. The localized expression is in turn an influence on the universal field as it enfolds from the explicate to the implicate. Our work includes consciously redesigning the beliefs that govern the dynamics of perception in our noetic energy field, not only because it affects *our own lives* but because it also affects, by enfolding, the implicate universal field as well.

In Husserl's model, cause is the a priori intentionality existing in the implicate order of Bohm's quantum universe. Causality, then, is always non-local. If something is local, it is effect. Local, in this sense, is the explicate, physical, space/time world. The way we affect change at the local level is to first change our relationship with life by moving our center of awareness from ego to soul, centering ourselves in the noetic, implicate world. As we do this, we gain the ability to transform our limitations, and to co-create with the universe. Thus, we master life, or rather we master our relationship to life. We become travelers through life's many dimensions, and thereby, through experience, transform our conflicts into enlightened understanding, which, in its completion, adds positive substance to our soul. Though we may begin our journey from an adversarial posture, we must resolve it through unification with the one universal whole.

## Nexus

A nexus is a means of connection, a tie or link. It is access. Physically and metaphysically, a nexus is a specialized cell or membrane that connects other cells, or realms of consciousness, to each other. Here, I am using the term to indicate a connection between neotic realities and the physical body, and between different dimensions, or orders, of noetic or implicate realities.

We create a nexus by placing and focusing our attention. When we hold a steady attention, an energy link condenses at that point. The consciousness we link to depends on our intention. The consciousness we seek to engage meets us at our point of

15

concentration, thus making the connection. The content of the intention determines the reality that we access. The technique of reduction creates a nexus by focusing and suspending our projections. In such a nexus, we are met by higher consciousness according to our capacity to receive it. One way we can meet a specific consciousness or frequency of noetic reality is by creating a visual image and focusing on that image as a singular event. This image can be an internal or external symbol, geometric form, color or sound.

The chakras are a nexus between physical and etheric levels. The use of these nexus points opens our higher sense perception, providing access to multidimensional experience and information. Points at the brow and top of head are particularly useful in this respect. To activate these connections, see a light in the center of your head and then extend the energy, through your intention, out the brow or top of your head. The meridians used in oriental healing are a type of nexus through which chi is translated for physical health.

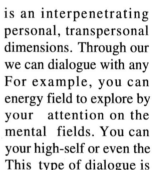

The noetic field is an interpenetrating consciousness of personal, transpersonal and universal dimensions. Through our focus, selective nexus, we can dialogue with any aspect of the noetic field. For example, you can choose what level of the energy field to explore by choosing and asserting your attention on the physical, emotional, or mental fields. You can focus your intention on your high-self or even the Christ, Buddha or Allah. This type of dialogue is like breathing in and breathing out. You speak whole heartedly and then you listen whole heartedly. Through your intention, you speak and then you listen. The "hearing" may be sound. More than likely, it will come as impressions, images, intuition, or knowing. When we regard one another with honor and respect, we initiate a deep, even intimate, level of rapport. The experience of rapport is due to the interfacing, or unifying, our individual noetic fields. Rapport, then, describes the nexus of our personal noetic fields. When we engage in this type of rapport, we may feel "presences" greater than ourselves. The experience of this presence indicates that our rapport is also a nexus with the universal noetic field. As we continue to engage each other through this personal and universal rapport, we may have the experience of moving with each other in a shared altered state of consciousness. We are able to have shared experiences of other dimensions of consciousness. When we are in a shared state of consciousness, we are better able to understand each other.

Good storytellers and charismatic teachers are masters of the expanded form or rapport, even if only intuitively. We can explore anything, through *inner* dialogue, by applying the same heuristic methods on an individual basis. A thing, a plant, a mineral, a state of consciousness, an idea, or even a topic of interest may be the focus of noetic discovery. In a classroom, or any setting where two or more are participating, the topic of interest becomes a shared focus. Through classroom rapport, teaching and learning can become a multidimensional experience.

## PRIMARY PERCEPTION

In the tradition of David Bohm, another physicist, Edward Close explores in his book, *Transcendental Physics,* the premise that, with the research that exists, modern science is obliged to shift from a materialist model of the universe in which consciousness is the result of material evolution to one that states that the material universe is the result of consciousness. In other words, consciousness is evolving the material universe for its own purposes. As a mathematical model for this process, Close developed what he calls a "calculus of distinction." If you have an interest in the notations of his calculus, refer to his book. For our purposes, I am bringing his work to this discussion because he makes the case from physics that, it is our observation that makes the reality possible.

Close suggests that a primary consciousness produces and sustains the universe as we know it. The simplest example of this is the "Double Slit" experiment, in which light observed one way appears as a particle and when observed another way it appears as a wave. The emphasis here is that light exists in a pre-observed state, and that depending on how we look at light, it appears as a wave or particle. This is called the *observer effect.* According to Close, this proves the necessity of developing a model for physics that includes conscious-ness. I ask that you seriously consider that we, as the perceiver, create our reality through a quantum dialogue with the universe. How this occurs remains a mystery. How to work it in terms of practical transformation is available to us, if you choose to embrace your role as co-creative agents.

Husserl, Bohm and Close share a common discovery: reality unfolds to us through our perception. We believe that reality is how it

17

seems. Bohm challenges this. There is a parallel between Close's proposition that the manifestation of the material form and energy depends on how we choose to observe it and Husserl's experience of transcendental reduction. Close states that consciousness is the final receptor that gives meaning to form. In effect, the final receptor is the same as the *observer*. We are a final receptor of consciousness. Conscious choice determines how energy appears as form. For example, light appears as a wave or particle, depending on how we choose to make our observations. The experience that Husserl called the noesis has the same attributes as what Close called the "final receptor." In healing terms, this is *witness*. It is as if there is a subtle level of particles that contain the electrical and magnetic qualities that are the foundation of our world. It is the unfolding of that particle level that creates our reality. Our perception appears to have direct impact on the unfolding of those particles.

Close's conceptualization of the nature of the universe is metaphorically similar to phenomenology in that we develop understanding through an ontology of distinctions evolving through the noetic methodology. Our perception is frozen in a matrix of sedimented beliefs. *Through transcendental reduction, the deconstruction of distinctions can take one to the ultimate source beyond which future reduction is impossible, or unnecessary.* This has direct application to the therapeutic process. The psychological issue is a belief system created by an individual, resulting from that person's quest for meaning. The definition of issue is that a held belief is not working. The belief is causing problems. It is a "disturbance in the Force." Life appears different when the "issue" is resolved. Changing the belief changes the reality for that person. The therapeutic activity is the same as Close's construct of the final receptor: *primary consciousness gives meaning to its own creation, as a witness.* While Close offers a calculus, Husserl offers a protocol by which we can experientially understand that calculus, and use it to transform our lives. At each context, we continue to circle deeper, until we reach the primary, a priori perception. This implies that the interlinking of creation is guided by "mathematical" formulae, and that these equations are activated by consciousness.

Our life began as a probability based on our inherent nature. It proceeds through a phase of false beliefs and addictions, and co-dependent hostilities. It begins to change when we choose deeper responses to life. As we identify with our emerging soul-centeredness, our perception shifts. At this point, we realize that we are a

collaborator with the one spirit that permeates all. Though an element of our learning, our attachment to guilt, blame and shame will cause us to miss the point. The point is that we live in a universe of contrast that teaches us discernment and choice. We learn to make distinction as a means of fulfilling consciousness.

*The conscious terminus is a function of an implicate, ordered holomovement.* According to Close, *creation knows itself in the conscious terminus of the non-quantum, non-material, non-local receptor.* The non-quantum receptor and the noesis (the I awareness) are the same. Primary consciousness contains the original distinctions that created the universe and is the unifying perception that organizes the universe. "In the beginning all was void, and God moved across the face of the deep and said let there be light." Thus, the sequence of distinctions that resulted in our lives at this time and place began. If it all began with "the word," we could say that the noetic terminus is the "last word," that our witness is the "last word." A last word that is continually spoken by our witness. In our perception, we choose how reality will unfold to us.

Close described the interface through which individual consciousness and primary or universal consciousness meet as a nexus. The noetic terminus (our awareness) is our nexus with primary consciousness. As the observer, we become non-locally aware, yet locally indexed. We are conscious of the explicate and implicate correlation simultaneously. We see the unity and the differentiation. Our observation collaborates with primary consciousness to facilitate

19

the unfolding and enfolding of the implicate and explicate orders. Transcendental reduction moves our awareness from material reality to non-local reality. Our observation unfolds the bridge between quantum and non-quantum reality. Close asserts that consciousness spawns material form. Phenomenology is analogous to the salmon swimming upstream. At some point in the deconstruction process, we consciously encounter primary consciousness, or the field of the Creator, in the form of its intention. When we form a nexus with our pre-choice, a priori, awareness, we are home.

## MAKING IT REAL

In my approach to psychology, therapy, and teaching the ability to be aware of *energy* is essential. Energy awareness becomes possible, by integrating our five senses with their multidimensional counterparts. Our bodies and the dynamic geometric etheric structures around it, form an expanded sensory array. They are the forms that shape the movement of energy. These energies interact with the electro-biological energy of our physical bodies. These systems interface and have a relationship with etheric systems. As we align these systems, channels for the flow of spiritual energy open. No matter what level or dimension, we are always working with a combination of context and relationship.

The chakras are centers of power and consciousness that interface with their physical counterparts. They also interface with etheric counterparts that appear as geometric structures around the physical body. The relationship of these fields is subject to our mental, emotional and imaginal activity. The following protocol will enable us to explore our innate capacity to enhance and transform our consciousness.

As we explore the following practices, our perception will shift and reframe our consciousness. This shift in context is a form of reduction that changes our perception of the noetic relationship between noema and noesis. This is a shift from a sense of self aligned with form to a sense of self aligned with essence.

### Eye Hand

Our bodies are bi-laterally symmetric. This forms a polarity, and when engaged in relationship, it generates an energy field that can be used to charge up the aura, or bio-electric field.

1.      Look at the palms of your hands as if you were holding a book at a distance of about a foot and a half from your face.

2.      Allow your arms and hands to relax, while maintaining their relationship to your eyes.

3.      After awhile, turn your hands so that the palms face each other.

4.      You may begin to feel something between your hands. Move your hands back and forth. It may feel like a spongy ball. You may feel heat, or an attraction.

5.      Push your hands together. As you rub your hands together you may hear a silky sound.

Looking at your hands builds an energy. Exploring the sensations of the field between your hands activates your awareness. Rubbing your hands together charges you energy field. You can repeat this exercise several time for stronger results. In this exercise the body and your hands form the context. The posture orients your centers to form the relationship that generates the energy. In a sense, the reductive focus and postures unfold, or move, the energy, or chi, from the implicate noetic field into the magnetic field of your body and expands into the aura.

## Rainbow

This exercise is the same as the Eye Hand, with the addition of color visualization. The visualization creates a nexus with that color vibration in the universal field. We use the visualization of colors often in later exercises. Each color is a creative force in the universe, governed by a conscious being with which we can converse. (*See Chohans of the Color Rays,* by John-Roger.) The purpose of this exercise is to balance your energy and strengthen your understanding, and awareness of energy. Do the entire sequence of the Eye Hand exercise with each color.

1.      While looking at your hands and facing your palms toward each other, visualize red and ask to be conscious and aware of

the being (Chohan) of red. You can form a dialogue and ask how red functions in the universe. Red is an energizing, generative color.

2.     Visualize orange. Orange is energizing, supportive, and sustaining.

3.     Visualize yellow. Yellow is mental energy and calms the mind.

4.     Visualize green. Green is healing.

5.     Visualize sky blue. Blue is the energy of Chi and elevates the consciousness.

6.     Indigo. Indigo sensitizes the psychic force-field.

7.     Purple. Purple energizes our soul relationship, and transcendental awareness.

8.     Silver. Silver grounds us and connects us to the cosmic flow of energy through the earth, and transcendentally to Source.

9.     Gold. Gold connects us to the source of love and power.

10.    Turquoise (blue-green). Turquoise connects us to the mediating power of source.

11.    White. White connects us to pure spirit and universal wisdom.

## Ra Hu

As corollary of the Rainbow exercise, I sometimes introduce the Ra and Hu chant as a means of activating and teaching the power of sound and energy.

1.     While doing the Rainbow Hand Eye exercise, chant "Ra" three times while visualizing orange. "Raaaaaaaaaa......" This will build energy and introduce you to the effects of Ra.

2.     While doing the Rainbow Hand Eye exercise chant "Hu" three times, while visualizing purple. "Huuuuuuuuuu...." This will

build transcendental energy and introduce you to the effects of Hu.

## Circle Energy

This is similar to the previous exercises except that it is done with a group. The purpose is to explore the power of the group as a conduit and generator of energy.

1. Form a circle with your group, holding your left hand palm up and parallel to the floor at your sides. Hold your right hand over the left hand of the person next to you. Hands are not touching. (This can be done with only two people by standing facing each other with hands in front of you at about waist level with your left hand turned palm up and your right hand palm down over your partner's left hand.)

2. At an even pace, the group visualizes each color, with an optional chanting "Ra" at orange and "Hu" at purple.

## Pushing Space

The universe meets us at our focus and responds to us with that which we pay attention to. In this exercise, we will explore the nature of energy, substance, and space. This exercise is for two or more people.

1. Sitting opposite one another, notice the air between you and how we take for granted that there is nothing in this space. Face your hands toward each other, moving them back and forth, noticing the movement through space.

2. Consider that when we are dreaming, reality is solid to our dream body. Attune to the reality that the air around you is solid. Move you hands toward each other. Notice subtle changes. Perhaps the shift is not so subtle.

Repeat the exercise with another person, one being passive and the other active. You can also do this as a group. One group pushes space and the other experiences the effect of that.

In Chi-gung, we attune our consciousness to the blue space around us, collecting chi through our movements. Also, consider that thought impacts the space around us. Other people's thoughts impact you as your thoughts may impact others, especially if you place emotional force or intent with the thought. What is good thought ecology for the space around us? Focusing with greater subtlety, we discover that "heaven is at hand."

*Nexus*

Basic to our inner awakening and perceptual acuity is our ability to activate our center, calling forward our holiness, and aligning with higher consciousness. Each of the following steps adds to the previous one, rather than doing one, dropping it and doing another. It is an additive sequence.

1.  See your body in the center of a sphere of light. This is your space. Call your holiness forward to fill your space.

2.  Place your attention in the center of your head. This is a reductive focus in which you set aside all expectation and thoughts. Hold your attention for at least three breaths.

3.  Place your attention high above the top of your head, and hold it there for three breaths, feeling your relationship to higher consciousness.

4.  Place your attention in your heart for three breaths.

5.  Look up at the star, or point of light that is at the top of your sphere, extend your focus to that point and engage the energy that is there. Invite universal holiness to fill your space. (An option is to journey through the star and after awhile bring the universal holiness into your space.)

6.  Relax and sustain your awareness, moving with any changes.

As we become more sensitive to the internal and external energy field, the noetic nature of human psychology becomes more apparent. As our bodies awaken to multidimensional awareness, we are increasingly capable of learning directly from our experience. Psychological issues arise from a separation, or blockage, in our ability to reflect on environmental events from the depth of soul. Health is restored or enhanced by a felt resonance between behavior, cognition, affect and our essence.

Time-bound, life appears linear. We may find our ancestor's foot prints baked in the mud on ancient shores. All that is significant occurs in the present moment. This is where time and implicate order intersect. It is in the moment that we find that our life story is merely the passing impression of our soul upon the surface of earth. We bind ourselves in time and begin our journey through the joy and suffering of life. We discover our divinity in the midst of our humanity. The personal, as we know it, is humble, a foot print of eternity. In the next chapter, we will explore the psychology of learning as a noetic phenomenon.

# REFERENCES

Bohm, D. *Wholeness and the Implicate Order.* New York: Routledge, 1998.

Close, E R. *Transcendental Physics.* Jackson, MO: Paradigm Press, 1997.

Harris, B, and J B Spurlock. *Paul Riceur: Key to Husserl's Ideas.* Milwaukee: Marquette University Press, 1999.

Ihde, D. *Experimental Phenomenology.* New York: Putnam, 1977.

## Chapter Two

# FOOT PRINTS

Intention is an act of perception. Life is the curriculum of the soul. Each moment is a foot print of eternity. When we actualize the full measure of the soul intent, learning is fulfilled, and the soul enhanced. As we discussed in Chapter One, Edmund Husserl developed "transcendental phenomenology" as a science of philosophy. He introduced a form of scientific rigor into philosophy. He did this by looking at the basic structure of experience. Normally, we organize our perceptions and the beliefs that inform our perception based on the appearance of the phenomenon itself.

Husserl discovered that by deconstructing the sedimented beliefs attached to a given phenomenon or thing, that his perception became altered and he found himself in a state of awareness that understood the movement of intentionality that was producing the thing. He called the thing *noema* and the intentionality *noesis*. He called his method "phenomenological reduction." In this view, essence moves toward discovery through the experience of form. Essence emerges into our awareness, as understanding, when the actualizing forces of essence-as-intentionality are freed by deconstructing the constellated beliefs.

I find this remarkable. Through the simple trust in his human capacity to experience, Husserl developed a systematic approach to understanding directly through experience. This is how life teaches us. In the thesis of this chapter, I call this type of learning *noegenesis*. The term *noegenesis* comes from the word noetic and means *apprehending new knowledge directly from experience*.

Husserl's protocol is "scientific" because the discovery occurs through the relationship (correlation) of indexed variables. Empirical science manipulates the relationship between two or more variables as a means of proving or disproving a hypothesis. Husserl manipulated his relationship to two variables in order to understand the *thesis* directly through experience.

Earlier, we discussed David Bohm's physics. In those terms, we see the *explicate* reality as objects and believe they are discrete. Bohm contended that "cause was not local." Cause is implicate. In this case, cause is *noesis,* and non-local. Husserl discovered a means by

27

which he could perceive the implicate order relative to any phenomenon he chose to explore. In the following discussion, we will further explore and apply Husserl's basic principles and refine our ability of *noegenesis*. In this way, we learn to track ourselves. We learn where we have been, where we are going, and who we are in the coming and going by tracking our *foot prints* through *eternity*.

## REDISCOVERING PRIMARY PERCEPTION

Spiritual discovery takes two paths. One is transcendental, in which we seek a direct experience with the Divine. We engage our holiness through an experience of revelation or enlightenment. We also seek the divine through creation. We seek an encounter of the sacred through the natural or phenomenal world.

The goal of Husserl's phenomenology was to understand. The protocols that he developed bear a close resemblance to yogic practices. The ancient mystery teaching looked at the "structure of experience" through sacred geometry, or the structure of reality.

### Reductive Focus Protocol

Husserl called the thing we want to understand, the thing as it appears, the "noema." The experience into which the understanding manifests, he called the "noesis." The noesis is the experience of the "I" that intuits the essence that correlates with the fact of the noema. The structure of experience is the correlation of intentionality as essence and form.

| noesis | noetic terminus | noema |
|---|---|---|
| ("I" essence intentionality) | (experiential correlation) | (fact) |

"Epoché" means to step back, to suspend our beliefs, or our usual ways of interpreting, or seeing. The steps to this process are called "phenomenological reduction" or "hermeneutic rules." I will expand these steps into a learning protocol. These steps give shape, focus, and direction to our investigation, interpretation, and learning.

**Step 1. Attending to the Phenomenon or Experience as it Appears.** This is the fact-stratum and constitutes a naive sense of given-ness. In other words, the object, or focus, is naively taken as it appears. We describe the phenomenon or experience and suspend all tendencies to explain. All phenomena within the limits of what is given are equal. At this stage, we bracket the phenomenon and temporarily exclude all belief and knowledge. We become naive.

**Step 2. Deconstruction.** The given-ness is loosened so that what appears to be empirically ordered shows itself to be the result of a tacit context of beliefs. A shift occurs in this process that expands our awareness. Our perceptual topography expands from a fact-stratum to include an essence-stratum.

**Step 3. Variations Are Explored.** Through these variations, any intentional aim is intuited or becomes evident. This type of intuition is exact. What is intuited is self-evident because it is demonstrated in the perception. Once one sees a variation or intentionality, there is no doubt that one has seen it. We look for invariants in the structures or features within the variation of the phenomenon or experience. The fundamental structure of experience is transcendental.

Said another way, in phenomenological reduction, we:

1) Focus on the thing, expression, or belief that we want to understand. In *quantum* terms this is a "distinction" or "explicated differentiation."

2) Bracket the phenomenon. Bracket means to exclude all else from attention except the phenomenon itself.

3) Deconstruct the localized belief, construct, or perceptual fixity regarding person, place, or things. This engenders an altered state of consciousness, that transports experience to a transcendental state.

4) In the transcendental, or noetic mind, the correlating intention or understanding of the phenomenon directly presents itself as an experience of apprehending the *truth*.

By following the above protocol, we learn *noegenetically*. When we learn *noegenetically*, we take care to have the best supporting context that will enable the intended learning. For example, when we are present, we create a supportive context. We can also create an environment that is conducive to being present. Further care brings deeper results. We work with the structure of experience within that context. The scope is multidimensional. The context, teacher, student, materials, and subject matter all have noematic correlations. That is, they each index to an intentionality. They are all fulfilling their natures and agendas. There are no real static participants, human or otherwise. The only way I have found to mediate all of these interests is through higher consciousness. That which seems like chaos implies a higher organization. There is a unifying field and by following the protocol, it will make itself evident to us. As abstract as this might seem at first there is a practicality. We can align our humanity with the field of life and life moves to resolves itself. When we are radically present, sufficient deconstruction occurs to promote spontaneous insights.

As we continue, our ability to see the correlation of outer form and intentional purpose will be made increasingly evident. At first the concepts and applications of the protocols and principles may seem difficult. My advice is to persevere. Your effort stimulates the spiritual organs that, in time, awaken the capacities that our exploration and discussion seeks to convey.

## Noetic Confluence

To engage the capacity of the soul as *inner teacher,* we must loosen the grip of the ego and its socialized limiting belief systems. We may begin by asking God, "Why?" In the analogy of boiling water, we have two answers. We can explain that the reason the water boils in a tea kettle is because the heat excites the molecules until the water boils. Or, we can say the water is boiling because we wanted a cup of tea. When we understand, the *why* is evident. Noetic learning bridges the implicate and explicate order of the subject matter in the experience of the student. From the noetic learning perspective, material learning is formed and limited by dualism. Dualism sees as either/or, this/that, for/against, etc. Dualistic approaches to discovery are adversarial, and facts are correlated with facts as a basis of inference. This is done, of course, in pursuit of the truth. In a noetic approach, we add to that a transcendental, or metaphysical, element. To illustrate, the dualistic nature of apparent distinctions form the base of a triangle.

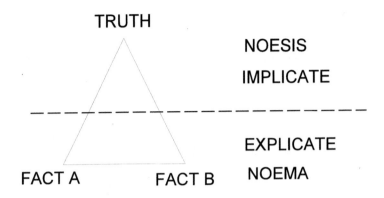

TRUTH

NOESIS

IMPLICATE

EXPLICATE

FACT A          FACT B          NOEMA

Bohm and Husserl suggest that the distinction is only apparent. Noesis and noema are not dualities. They are best understood as the apex of a triangle. The noema is seen as relating to other noema: fact vs. fact. Noema are the two lower points of the triangle and the apex is the noesis. In noetic learning, we are working with a trinity.

As in the ancient mystery teachings, Husserl's methods change the consciousness of the practitioner. It's like a Western yoga, a training for mystical understanding overlaid by the Western need for scientific rigor. He is not alone in this. As practitioners of noegenetic learning, we are participating in the same wisdom. We are applying and responding to the same set of skills. The well being of the student and the adeptness of the practitioner are effects of the same grace.

F J Hanna points out, in *The Journal of Transpersonal Psychology*, that ... *in Husserl's scheme, it would appear that such individual being's core boundaries are 'interpenetrated' forming a kind of transpersonal confluence in which there is a simultaneous, dialectical unity and separation of individual beings.* (Hanna, p 185). Hanna elaborates on the similarity of the transcendent state described by Husserl as that of absolute being, recapitulating the steps of Patanjali's yoga: "concentration," "contemplation," and "realization." Aspects of transcendental phenomenology are also reflected in Steiner's *Higher Worlds and Its Attainment*. He prescribes a similar training of will and focus as a way to develop the mind as an organ of spiritual perception.

Noetic learning harkens to the prophetic projections of Sri Aurabindo and Teilhard de Chardin. Aurabindo's perspective emerged from the Eastern yogas as the coming nexus of the mind of humanity with the supramental realm. Chardin called this realm the "noussphere" and believed that humanity's grasp of this realm is an emergent evolutionary potential.

## Elements for Internal Union

The heart and the mind, as we are accustomed to those centers, awaken together to form a noetic energy-field. The impetus to learn is much like the archetype of the Beloved. Our longing for home, wholeness, and soulmate is the a priori intention motivating us to explore and to understand. Love provides the intimacy and trust that is most like the nature of the Creator and the essence of intentionality. In the noetic relationship, love touches deeper and engenders dialogue. This loving is unconditional in the cosmic sense. It is the love of the Divine Mother. The will and focus are the Divine Father.

The intentionality of noegenetic learning is discovery, understanding, and fulfillment. We are father and mother. Within this union, our will and love can awaken healing, bring forth the truth, create dialogue, and touch the living energy of our environment. In this internal union, we are invited into the mysteries. As said by Saint Paul, "Let the mind that is in Jesus be in us." The resolution, fulfillment and understanding of life is the progeny.

George Washington Carver is an intriguing example of noegenetic thinking. He could see through appearance into the essence of things. His mind-set, structure of mind, or noetic nature enabled him to open to direct perception. He knew that each thing has its nature and that all we need do is see it and ask the purpose (intentionality) of its creation. Carver is well known for his work at Tuskegee Institute. He was a practical scientist whose discoveries made a significant contribution to the agricultural economy of the South. His many discoveries for the use of peanuts are especially noted. His approach was first to speak with the essence of the plant and then detail in the laboratory what he perceived. Christopher Bird called him the man who talked with plants. The laboratory results were then applied as a material science. Carver was convinced that God created and sustained the universe, and he conducted his science accordingly. (Bird).

Is perception generated by the intentionality of a creator or by our mind-set? The history of church and science is full of such debate. The noetic perspective invites us to consider that our reality comes from our relationship with the physical and transcendental universe.

God seems to respond according to our ability to understand. The human potential to converse with the Divine is progressive and evolutionary. It increases as we generate and resolve history. Jesus said that "... we will do the things I do and even greater things." Given that Jesus exhibited a high degree of mastery, the implication of such a statement is profound. In his way, Buddha encouraged us to achieve enlightenment, and discover our Buddha-Nature.

In other words, the universe was created out of an agency, or primary consciousness, out of a noetic field. Charles Darwin saw the foot prints of the Creator and believed the ontology came out of the form and did not consider agency. On the other hand, the creationist has difficulty with the possibility that the Creator (agent) is actualizing itself through the Creation as a Darwinian protocol.

This calls to account the nature of fact and truth, which are not necessarily synonymous or as congruent as science and religion would like to believe. Noetic learning invites us to engage facts reflectively and relationally as a means of discovering the truth. Perhaps scriptures were edited as an attempt to dominate the divine intelligence, and subsume it under the material mind. If creation is acting through us, the urge to material domination is a limiting and immature expression of an intention toward co-creative mastery. We, as human kind, have the same creative potential as a "Christ-class" (Buddha -class...Laot-se-class, etc.) human being. Can we accept that in ourselves?

## *Transdualism*

When we speak of the Dao, we think of the rhythm of yin and yang as it unfolds through time, place, and circumstance. That is the mind. Dao is called the way. Yet in truth, it precedes "the way." It is the essence of love that is unity itself, beyond itself. We know it as a fragrance, a presence, a sweet melody that makes life. When we consider the truth of universal love that precedes the yin and yang, we have instead a model for creation as a basic tripartite particle structure out of which all more complex structures are derived.

The term transdualism provides a means to explore dualism in a context of unity. "Non-dualistic" implies the exclusion of dualism, which is subtly dualistic. When we experience our dualism within a larger field of awareness, we have not made ourselves separate or exclusive; we have a distinction within wholeness. John Welwood describes this as a dialectic progression.

*Before becoming self-reflective, we are identified with the thoughts, beliefs, feelings, and memories arising in consciousness, and this keeps us imprisoned in conditioned mind. With reflection, we can start to free ourselves from the unconscious identifications by stepping back and observing them. Yet as long as we are stepping back, we remain in a state of divided consciousness. A further step would be to go beyond reflection and, without falling back into prereflective identification, become at-one with our experiencing —through overcoming all struggle with it, through discovering and abiding in the deep, silent source from which all experience arises. This third level of the dialectic, which takes us beyond most Western psychological models and philosophical frameworks, is post-reflective—in that it usually follows from a ground-work of reflective work—and transreflective—in that it discloses a way of being that lies beyond divided consciousness. (Welwood, p 116).*

Welwood goes on to say that phenomenology, ... *which, in emphasizing subject-object interrelatedness, is one of the most refined, least dualistic Western ways of exploring human experience, usually fails to go this further step.* (Welwood, p 116). I believe some of this is because in Western psychology the place of mysticism has not been fully acknowledged or integrated into our philosophy of learning. Whereas, in some aspects of Eastern approaches, the mystical, spiritual, psychological, and educational aspects are enfolded into the same philosophy of learning. While dualism may have provided ambition, it appears to withhold fulfillment. I would also suggest that being-one-with is a form of deconstruction and the ultimate state of noesis includes and transcends all noema.

What this leads me to consider is that transdualism is an emergent developmental phenomenon, as observed by Steiner, Joseph Chilton Pearce, Aurabindo, and Chardin. Although transdualistic love, as an expression of spiritual intelligence, has the attention of some of us, both East and West, it appears to me that adversarial protocols for resolving conflict are often preferred.

In the transdual experience, understanding is direct and accessible without the need to access such awareness through reflection. Welwood calls this a "nondual presence." He states, *In this unified field of presence, neither perceptions nor awareness can be objectified as anything the mind could grasp.* (Welwood, p 117). In the following, the "unified field of presence" is an attribute of what I call the *noetic field.* The implication is that the field nature of the consciousness, as experienced, is the essence of love and intelligence itself. This appears to be what the Buddhists call "emptiness." Welwood describes it in this wonderful statement:

> *Emptiness in this sense is not some "attribute" belonging to awareness, appearance, or being, but their utter transparency when apprehended in pure presence, outside of the subject/object framework. . . . As self-illuminating awareness that simultaneously illumines the whole field of experience, pure presence is intimate engagement, rather than a stepped-back detachment. In contrast to reflection, it does not involve any "doing" at all. (Welwood, p 117).*

At this stage our "ambition" becomes fulfillment. Yet, is ambition gone? Or, is it enfolded into the pure presence and experience as fulfillment? In Christian terms, we speak of being one with the will of the ...[Creator]. Being one with, we are doing nothing. Life is actualizing itself and we are congruent with that. So, fulfillment can be seen as ambition without separation. Epoche' may also be a form of detachment or centering. Noesis in my experience is not disengagement.

I refer to this consciousness as soul-space or soul presence. The experience of this consciousness is what I call *noegenesis.* Though soul is not a Buddhist concept, when one is aware in the way described, who cares? Any strategy in the phases of therapy or learning preceding this stage of pure presence is intended to transform and transmute forces that compete with one's gravitational relationship to center, soul-space, or emptiness. From my perspective, issues are an invitation to this transdual field of consciousness. Once one welcomes such a state, transmutation and transformation follow from the continued flow of that experience.

Another aspect of the transdual state is what Jesus called being in the world but not of it. In Eastern terms, this is called "liberation." In the transdualistic field, we are no longer shaped by our thought, feeling, trauma, or belief of others. Although these factors may shape our interactions with others, we exist as transparency and as divine presence with the larger field of our awareness and activity. Doing unfolds being and being enfolds doing. The enlightened being is qualitatively different. Through many cycles of being and doing, it now has the ability to consciously unfold into doing, at will, rather than because it must or cannot.

## Observational Construction

Len Flier, in *The Journal of Transpersonal Psychology*, offers an insightful perspective on how we might construct our psychospiritual nature in terms of constructive-developmentalism. Flier's perspective echoes Bohm's discussion on *structation,* which means "to structure." Structation is a process of unfolding form or, in Close's terms, distinction. Flier poses the question: Is our deep nature inherent or constructed?

*As a developmental model of basic structures of consciousness, constructive-developmentalism represents a departure from models based on metaphors of "activation" or "unfolding." The perennial philosophy—expressed as yoga chakras, for example—has been interpreted to mean that preexisting or latent orders of consciousness are sequentially "awakened" by spiritual practice. Constructive-developmentalism, however, says that such consciousness structures do not exist until they are constructed by the individual. The appropriate metaphor for the development of consciousness, then, is not awakening, but evolution. Just as Darwin would say that there is no "latent zebra" hidden in the deep structures of the Earth, constructive-developmentalism says that there is no "latent fifth-order of consciousness" hidden in the deep structures of the individual. Zebras evolved in a specific ecosystem as a response to a specific set of environmental challenges. Likewise, an order of consciousness evolves in a specific individual as a response to a specific set of ontological challenges. Although a theory of the evolution of consciousness could prove as hard for theology to swallow as a theory of the evolution of life, I think there is much*

36

*more agreement than disagreement between constructive-developmentalism and religion, and I believe that a theory of the evolution of consciousness can be viewed as a vindication of the perennial philosophy rather than as a challenge. (Flier, 149).*

The debate between whether we awaken deep structures or construct them, though interesting, may miss the mark. A rule of thumb, that has served me well, is that when it comes to either/or, it is probably both. It appears that one of the functions of DNA is to balance environmental conditions with spiritual imperatives. Our physical and psychological bodies are the resolution. If that is the case, we have a deep structure (essence) responding to an environmental challenge. Consequently, our consciousness is the result.

Close points out that a light registers as a wave or a particle depending entirely on how we choose to observe it. Does that mean, as the constructionist would say, that light was constructed by the observer? Probably not. Yet, its appearance occurred from the interplay of our consciousness and the potential of light. There is something in the latent structure that responds to the observation. Perhaps the latent form in the deep structure is formed by what Close calls "primary consciousness." Evolution then is a collaboration between primary consciousness (God), environmental circumstances, and the sentient being involved. We can conclude then that each perspective is assessing one aspect. Observation did not make light, and our developmental construction did not make our spiritual potential. In both cases, however, observation and construction influences the nature of how the phenomenon appears in the physical world. Our innate spiritual potential contains the will to unfold into form. For it to do so, we invite the unfolding. There is "nothing to swallow." That viewpoint comes from the level of mind that holds our perception in a dualistic framework. As we construct our mind-set, our holiness awaits our invitation as a "deep structure."

What is our relationship with creation and the Creator? A unity view suggests that we construct personality through choice based on latent structures. One level was formed through evolution, and a deeper level was formed by the Creator. Jesus said to Peter, "What you bind on earth is bound in heaven" and vice versa. In other words, development emerges from a reciprocity of the observer and nonlocal or spiritual reality. This fits Bohm's model as the local enfolds into the universal and the universal unfolds into the local. What excites me is that Flier, in the discussion of constructive-developmentalism, says that the way we exist locally, as form, is affected by our choices. Is "awakening" a means of "constructing?" In an analogous way, Close points out that the wave or particle nature of light depends on the choices we make in our method of observation. The light was doing something before we observed it. It had a deep structure with a potential to be particle or wave. Our observation decided which way it would appear. Over the years, I have found that when we are confronted with two contrasting options, that the answer is usually: both.

## NOEGENESIS

Noegenetic learning embraces the goals and content of traditional education. The difference is in how we develop our perception and how we understand ourselves as learners and mentors. From the noetic perspective:

- Education is soul-centered.

- All endeavor serves the realization, actualization, and care of this sacred embodiment.

- Life supports life, which enables us to live sustainable, environmentally generative lives.

Our personal tasks are:

- To master the noetic transformation of our minds.

- To understand and apply the two aspects of the noegenetic nature of learning:

    - a) how to experientially apprehend new knowledge, and

    - (b) how to derive old knowledge as experientially new to the learner.

- To understand and negotiate our symbiotic relationship with the noetic field.

The learning protocol is applicable to a variety of learning and therapeutic settings. I developed it to help us engage any aspect of the curriculum, whether didactic or experiential. As we use the protocol to understand and learn, it serves not only to enhance our ability to use it, but also, as a yoga and spiritual or noetic practice in and of itself, as a means of developing our acuity.

Everything is essentially an energy of infinite variation until we make contact; then it becomes a noetic field that supports and responds to the focus that engaged it. In our case, we experience reality as a response to our focus. This is the same protocol as the "double-slit" experiment in which light appears as wave or particle, depending on our mode of observation. Contact is a mode of observation. The implicate order unfolds its noetic nature on our contact. Further unfolding occurs based on the implication of our focus. Our interest and focus creates a configuration in the noetic field. This invites a noetic response, which then occurs in the form of symbolic meaning that we can understand. Once we contact the noetic field, it responds congruently at our level of consciousness. Everybody's symbology is confirmed. The truth is in the relationship.

The learning protocol will open your perception into a noetic state. It is a *trans-dual* awareness that encompasses duality and transcends into a larger perceptual field. This state of higher sensory awareness is similar to Husserl's transcendental ego. It is excellent preparation for study, research, dialogue with a client, or exploration with students. The protocol is a way to experientially access the essence that correlates with the given issue, topic, thing, substance, or fact. It enables you to move from the fact-stratum to the essence-stratum. It provides a way to journey with a class, client, or colleague. Use the protocol to guide learning or therapy in relationship to a topic or issue. You can also use it as a meditation practice or research guide.

**Step 1. Alignment.** Choose and engage the focus, paying attention and relaxing, breathing and engaging, centering and aligning focus with higher consciousness. This can be enhanced by observing your physical body in the center of a sphere of energy and holding your attention in the center of your head.

**Step 2. Bracketing.** Focus forward in the perceptual field and describe it as it appears; exclude any distraction, suspend all tendencies to explain, and exclude all beliefs and knowledge. Bracketing perceptually contains the noema in preparation for the next step.

**Step 3. Deconstruction.** Regard all aspects of the presenting phenomenon as having equal value. Step back into a perspective of observer such that you are no longer dependent on what is observed for your definition or safety, or for its definition.

Sedimentation is the unstated context or belief that results in the given phenomenon appearing as being empirically ordered or perceptually fixed due to our conditioning, agreement, and belief. The process of deconstructing is often referred to as transcendental reduction or epoché. There are many ways to deconstruct, such as cognitive dissonance, multiple viewpoint, metaphor, varying context, multiple observer, altered state, reframing, self-forgiveness, seeing as energy.

**Step 4. Intuition.** Experience the self-evident, intuitive response of the intention or meaning of the given focus phenomenon. Experience the truth that correlates to the fact. The deconstruction has taken you into a transcendental state of knowing. Your reflexive action moved you into an experience of the noesis.

**Step 5. Elaboration.** The intuition or knowing will guide you as the noesis unfolds into your awareness. The experience of perception is a movement of noetic intelligence which replaces conventional material thinking. As a means of elaboration choose from the following approaches. This approach unfolds or attracts illumination. In this way the noema is a point of entry, an index that selects which noesis unfolds. It is similar to the phenomenon of seeing light as wave or particle depending on the means of observation. In this way we can speak of the noesis as a correlation to the noema.

*Gestalt:* Using the noesis as a theme, begin to gather through research, discussion, or observation bits of information via symbol, image, sensation, and frequency until a gestalt emerges or a knowing precipitates directing your further understanding of the noesis.

*Traveling:* Through stream of consciousness, association, guided imagery, or contemplation with the noesis, see where it takes you.

*Dialogue:* Using the noema as the topic or as a life form, ask questions, respond, and pursue through discussion. In other words, dialogue with the noema or with someone or others about the noema.

**Resonance:** Truth and the elaboration of truth is found through resonance. *Resonance* is a sympathetic vibration between two wave forms or distinct frequencies. In electronic metaphor, like-frequencies in matched systems can transfer power or energy and information through induction. In psychological metaphor, this is empathy.

**Step 6. Epiphany.** Experience the realization or further insight. When the answer and the question intersect, we experience a realization. Epiphany is a further insight in which the *light* comes to the context that our elaboration created. Epiphany comes from a deeper or more transcendental noetic stratum than the noema and noesis reflections.

**Step 7. Mystery.** Symbolize your topic and place it, for example, on an altar, in the hand of God, into a field of energy, in your own hands. Wherever you metaphorically put it, see it dissolve into light. This technique transfers the vibratory pattern (noesis) from your noetic field to the universal noetic field. The universal noetic field takes it, responds in its own way, and returns it to you plus the evolution, transformation, or metamorphoses, that occurred through its universal journey.

Illumination, transparency, and ecstacy can lead to the conclusion that we have arrived. Husserl stopped at the experience of his "a priori intentionality." Others stop at the *transintentional* experience of nirvana or divine presence. With the risk of proposing a new duality, I invite you to consider that since we discovered more of the self in order to get where we are—no matter how great that is—there may be more. In the meantime, we can "send a probe." I hope duality has not become a bad word. We can consider an aspect of any noetic field as a mystery. The mystery is sufficiently deconstructed so it is unlike the noema. For this stage, we need a noetic device that will allow us to translate our epiphany or noesis into the field of the mystery, even though we may only have a theory, report of someone else's experience, or a spiritual teaching to tell us what its characteristics are. Of course, these models are helpful. In a sense, we are imposing a device into what appears to be nothing, emptiness, or everything for the purpose of awareness. To do this step, we must choose some symbolic form for the mystery. This leaves us with the

41

bench mark that our higher awareness is a subtle reflection that obscures any further multidimensional reality through the appearance of emptiness. Not to worry, send your message.

**Step 8. Response.** Experience any further comment or realignment the mystery makes in whatever form.

**Step 9. Integration and Adaptation.** Understanding gained through experience changes the noetic field. While the soul adapts quickly, the basic self needs longer to adjust. It must adapt to the new. The boundaries of survival, safety, and nurture accommodate the transformation. We may have to live with these changes as we adjust. At times we can feel disoriented

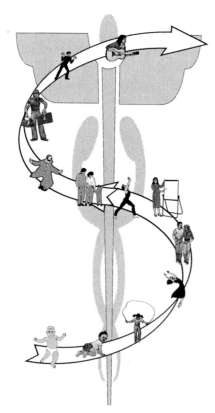

**Step 10. Circularity.** Start again with Step 1 of the learning protocol using your new focus.

The learning curve is complete. Noetic learning is spiral. By that I mean that we acquire aspects of a topic on progressive levels. If it is a competency, we cycle around, refining it at each new level. If it is knowledge or understanding, we progressively deepen, refine and elaborate it at each higher octave of the spiral. In linear learning, there is a beginning and an accomplished goal that signifies completion. These two ways of learning are not antithetical. The linear is imbedded in the circular. Learning brings one to a higher level of consciousness. The learning experience changes the learner personally, spiritually, and substantively.

At each level, the new turn of the spiral begins the sequence again, because the purpose of learning is to advance the essence of the learner. The only constant is the ever increasing experience level of the soul. Understanding must be deconstructed and reintegrated at each increasingly subtle turn of the spiral. Maturity is gauged by the assimilation of knowledge, understanding, and skill into essence. We occur as a parallel event within the spiral. From this perspective, the learning spiral is the noema and the soul axis is the noesis. We become more like the mystery with the added feature of our noetic capacity to be individually conscious of the universality. We are the universal mystery, individually aware.

## Building Blocks

We build structures of consciousness through protocols. The protocols are sequences of experiences that form, transform, combine, or integrate units of energy. For example, we act out of unconscious or conscious intentions, encounter a response, reflect on that response, make a choice or decide something about ourselves, which then becomes a belief about the way we are or life is. That is a protocol. The exercises in these chapters are also examples of protocols. In this chapter, we further explored the *reductive protocol* of phenomenology and *noegenetic* learning. In the coming chapters, we will continue to refine our skill and understanding of protocols.

The migration from ego to soul-centered thinking is gradual. Many small subtle shifts produce quantum shifts. We easily notice the quantum shifts, because we have sudden epiphanies or shifts in perception, clarity, wholeness, loving or intelligence. The subtle, incremental shifts require a more refined discernment. As we internalize the guidance of Husserl, we find a natural comfort with one foot in noema (the world) and one foot in noesis (heaven). We live in a correlational reality that generates an evolving spiral of experience and understanding. Learning is circular and progressive.

Through reflection and enquiry, our senses extend, giving us a direct contact with the actual reality implied by the model. In a sense, the model is symbolic language that carries the frequencies of the realities, providing a means of attunement and access. We develop the skill of modeling, which is a collaboration between our evolving capacity to understand and perceive, and our affinity with the levels of our consciousness that exist in these realities. We can use this material to develop our capacity to form and implement the benefits of our *spiritual anatomy.*

As we step upon the damp earth, we leave an impression. The animated body leaves its mark, a foot print. What of wholeness? The animated soul enshrouds itself in light and travels upon the winds of cosmic melodies to journey among the stars and venture into the possibility of self and caress the face of God.

# REFERENCES

Aurobindo, S. *The Future Evolution of Man: The Divine Life Upon Earth.* Wheaton, IL: The Theosophical Publishing House, 1974.

Chardin, P T. *The Future of Man.* New York: Harper & Row, 1964.

Dukes, S. "Phenomenological Methodology in the Human Sciences." *Journal of Religion and Health, vol 23, no 3, Fall 1984.*

Flier, L. "Demystifying Mysticism: Finding a Developmental Relationship Between Different Ways of Knowing." *The Journal of Transpersonal Psychology, Vol 281, no 2, 1996.*

Hanna, F J. "Rigorous Intuition: Consciousness, Being, and the Phenomenological Method." *The Journal of Transpersonal Psychology, vol 25, no 2, 1993.*

*Chapter Three*

# SPIRITUAL ANATOMY

Models help us understand. In some ways they resemble mythology. Like metaphor and myths, models provide symbolic connection between our hearts, minds, and archetypal depth. Throughout the ages, dedicated individuals developed the ability to refine their sensibilities and create maps for the human psyche. In this chapter, we will compare various models that reflect universal themes about human nature. The exercise of doing so develops our ability to make associations and see relationships. The practice of making models expands our perceptive range. Models never encompass everything, so we are actually engaged in an alchemical process of which we are the outcome.

As a conceptual foundation, we will explore the relationship between the "three selves" models of Huna and Psychosynthesis, and the "functional centers" approach, using the example of the chakras and Maslow's Hierachy of Needs. The key is to use your imagination and feelings. These models are abstraction that reflect the organization of real dynamic structures and systems that organize and direct energy in specific ways, yet, doing so, while implicated in a whole, universal system. After exploring these models, we will practice applied techniques, based on the three selves. In the study of *spiritual anatomy*, of course, the map is not the territory. I invite you to go beyond the scope of this writing to explore the dynamic relationship of your DNA to your subtle bodies and the corresponding psychological implications of that connection. To do that, you will have to imagine what that relationship would look like. Imagine yourself inside your DNA and then project that image into a geometric form surrounding and containing your physical body.

## HUNA

The Huna model comes from the Hawaiian wisdom of the Kahuna. This indigenous teaching shares many characteristics with ancient teachings throughout the world. As a practical teaching for non-indigenous people, it was first popularized on the mainland by Max Freedom Long, and, then, subsequently by native teachers. The key to spiritual alignment is the agreement between the "three selves," and the use of subtle energy through the mastery of that relationship. The three selves are: *basic self, high self,* and *conscious self.*

## Basic Self

The *basic self* is noncreative and contains our inculturated memories, the archetypal pattern of our destiny, our inner child, the seat of body intelligence, and the will to survive.

Its job is to maintain the status quo. In other words, the basic self has assimilated the beliefs developed through our life span and believes we will die if we change them. It will, however, respond to our authority and yield to any transformation that facilitates the actualization of our destiny. We contact the high self through the basic self.

Carolyn Myss' teaches that our family patterns, social norms, and mores are held in these lower centers and govern the higher ones until we transform our addictions, resolve our conflicts, and reclaim our center. In Huna, the power of the basic self increases as the internal divisions and beliefs that run contrary to one's nature are resolved. As a focus of healing, one must hold a clear image of the pattern that needs healing or, of the prayer one wants to have answered. This image is then charged with the energy of the basic self through breathing, emotion, and force of will and then surrendered to the high self. This is a similar technique to prayer and affirmation.

## High Self

The *high self* is creative and noninflictive. As a "guardian angel," it links us with our soul, the universe, and the high self of others. Because the high self exists in a spiritual dimension, it cannot violate anyone or anything. Even if the high self has better wisdom, it will not supersede our conscious self choice unless we ask it to.

We speak to it courteously and reverently. It is the authorizing agent for our ability to forgive ourselves. The high self takes the charged image from the basic self and amplifies that energy until healing, or the answer to the prayer, can be delivered into psychological and physical levels. In the wisdom of the high self, prayers are answered in a form that is for the highest good of everyone involved. This can be viewed as our personal connection to our higher power in 12-step terms.

## Conscious Self

The *conscious self* is our waking life. It is creative and innocent until a choice is placed into action. Its function is to be the vanguard of new experience. In the conscious self, we make choices and gain skill. As we grow in awareness and spiritual illumination, we extend the conscious self and become increasingly able to live in the awareness of the high self and be conscious of the dynamics of the basic self.

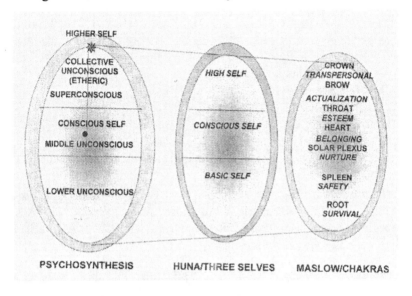

PSYCHOSYNTHESIS          HUNA/THREE SELVES          MASLOW/CHAKRAS

# PSYCHOSYNTHESIS

Through the resolution of conflict and competing interest in the internalized family, tribe, and nonintegrated aspects of self, a synthesis occurs that facilitates alignment with the high self.

An interesting feature of Assagioli's work is that it came from his study of the Alice Bailey material. Bailey was a spiritual teacher who developed a broad-based spiritual psychology from material she received as a transcendental teaching from a source she called The Tibeten. Her system is intricate and esoteric. Assagioli articulated selected aspects of her esoteric psychology into a practical psychology that was more accessible to conventional psychology and psychotherapy while carefully maintaining the spiritual core. Remarkably, it shares many features with the Huna/Three Selves model.

*Lower Unconscious* contains the intelligence that controls bodily function and survival and complexes developed through our emotional responses, memories, and incomplete or imbalanced expression, such as phobias, obsessions, compulsive urges, and paranoid delusions.

*Middle Unconscious* assimilates new and ordinary encounters, such as gestation, formulation of preconscious thinking, and meditative processes.

*Higher Unconscious-Superconscious* is the area of spiritual energies and ethical values. Intuition and conscious connection to the higher self are mediated in this area. Inspiration in all areas emanate from this area. It is our source of joy and altruistic love.

*Higher Self* is the transcendent self (indicated as a star) that exists even when we are unconscious. It is our eternal center from which our personality expression emanates and returns.

*Collective Unconscious* is the unconsciousness collective of humanity. In the diagram our personal field is shown as an oval. The oval represents a membrane that defines our space and serves as an interface with the collective consciousness.

*Field of Consciousness* is the Conscious Self. The flow of life that forms our immediate awareness. The conscious self is our point of self-awareness. The conscious self functions within our field of consciousness.

## MASLOW

Maslow believed that a hierarchy of needs governed our motivation. Like Huna and Psychosynthesis, these needs are progressive, from survival to transpersonal. As we are able to fulfill the need of each ascending level, we are then able to respond to the need of the next level. For example, concern for our *safety* is possible after we have assured our *survival*. *Nurture* is possible when we experience *safety*.

We can turn to *transpersonal* concerns when we have *self-esteem* and are able to *actualize* our goals in life. The transformation of the hierarchy of needs is enhanced as we awaken and identify with our transpersonal or soul self.

**Survival:** Meeting the basic requirement of staying alive.

**Safety:** Free from harm or the threat of harm.

**Nurture:** Receiving sufficient physical and emotional food to function in a healthy way.

**Belonging:** Being a functional and emotional part of a group of people with common interests and goals.

**Esteem:** Having a good self-concept, and feeling that one's nature is good, lovable, and that one is effective in one's life.

**Actualization:** Fulfillment of one's personal interests, inherent nature, and potential.

**Transpersonal or Meta:** Realization and awakening to one's spirituality and impulses that transcend personality and that arise out of a need for wholeness.

## CHAKRA

Just as Maslow developed his hierarchy of needs by observing individuals' motivation and scope of living, ancient mystics in India observed human expression and structure, which resulted in the coherent chakra system of yoga psychology.

The chakras are vortexes of energy that coordinate, shape, and direct the flow of our consciousness. They interact with each other depending on personality type, interest, and lifestyle. Any one of the chakras can dominate the others as a unifying principle or executive office. Different chakras may also dominate different ages, making the chakra model a variation of developmental psychology.

Myss describes how our family and culture may dominate our spiritual potential. Typically, conditioning in the first three chakras is directed toward family, tradition, and society. When these patterns are

# Chakra Function

| CHAKRA | ARCHETYPE | FUNCTION |
|---|---|---|
| CROWN | Healing<br>Beauty<br>Inspiration | • connection to spiritual realms and source of manifestation<br>• we are individualization of universal love |
| BROW | Imagination<br>Discernment<br>Knowledge<br>Intuition<br>Wisdom | • bridge to higher consciousness or psychic domination and manipulation<br>• spiritual bridging vs spiritual ceiling<br>• test of the enlightened ego |
| THROAT | Will Power<br>Truthfulness<br>Communication<br>Creativity | • abuse of expression inhibits honoring our deepest feelings, truth, and creativity<br>• willingness to receive nurturing, food, sustenance vs addiction to substance or external agenda<br>• consciousness vs unconsciousness |
| HEART | Peace<br>Harmony<br>Love<br>Brotherhood<br>Sisterhood | • soul food<br>• source of happiness and joy<br>• sweetness and goodness<br>• core of person and essence of relationship |
| SOLAR PLEXUS | Choice<br>Self-Worth<br>Confidence<br>Power | • personal identity and power<br>• dependency on need attachments<br>• giving pieces away for validation<br>• assimilating support and sustenance from the environment |
| SACRAL | Well-Being<br>Sexuality<br>Pleasure<br>Abundance | • sexual abuse<br>• psychic survival vs creativity<br>• scarcity vs abundance<br>• sadomasochism vs pleasure |
| ROOT | Patience<br>Structure<br>Stability<br>Security<br>Manifestation<br>Order | • collective thoughts, tribe, clan, race, family, genetics<br>• financial loss, poverty, uprootment, life-threatening crisis, war<br>• strong religious feelings, instinctive suppression |

transformed, authority is released into the higher centers. Various yogic practices aid in the development of the chakras. As each center is mastered in an ascending order, the next higher chakra can safely awaken.

The relationship between the development of the chakras and developing psychological help through Maslow's hierarchy is evident. The yogic systems and practices go further than Maslow did in that each chakra accesses a resource of psychic or spiritual energy. As these energies are developed and integrated, one's mastery of life, personal power, spirituality, multidimensional awareness, intuition, and psychospiritual seeing are enhanced. Maslow expressed this energy as the intentional flow of each need, as an actualization of self. As the chakras are opened and balanced, an energy called "kundalini" rises through the ascending centers. This energy eventually reaches the crown chakra (Maslow's level of transpersonal need) and connects to the transcendental levels of spiritual reality. According to Maslow, then, we have a need to balance and awaken these innate energies and fulfill their potentials. We experience this drive as the fulfillment of needs. Some forms of yoga strive to awaken the crown and brow chakras first as a means of transforming the lower ones. From this perspective, the transpersonal and actualizing centers strive to express equally and horizontally through all the chakras.

The diagram of the chakras on page 116 depicts an eighth and ninth chakra. In literature on the chakra, many more are often shown. The purpose here is to indicate our relationship to earth and grounding. The eighth chakra reflects place and issue of belonging in one's own life or on the planet. The ninth chakra extends the concept of transpersonal into a sense of a being that is transcendent. The practices in Surat Shabda Yoga and soul transcendence, invite travel into spiritual realms in one's soul body, as distinct from high self. This is a state of *soulness* that travels out of the body. It is a higher integration and distinctly not dissociation. As higher order of integration occurs the chakras merge, and the noetic functions of the microcosm and macrocosm begin to coordinate.

## QUIMBY

The roots of my experience with the aura and energy work comes from Phineaus Parkhurst Quimby, through Dr. Hunter. Though Quimby preceded Long, Assagioli, Maslow, and Myss, his approach combines many of these elements into what he called the "Science of the Christ." To him the Christ was a personally centered core self, forming a nexus with the *universal Christ*. Illness, disease, or psychological distortions were caused by beliefs that block the Christ-energy. In his sessions, he explained the nature of healing, and explored the blocking beliefs with the client. Then he would work with them silently. In the silent phase, he aligned with the Christ and witnesses. The revelation of the "truth"centered the client and engaged the inner Christ, providing the transforming witness. Quimby was one of the American Transcendentalist, along with Ralph Waldo Emerson and others, who brought a spiritual vision into the formation of the "American Philosophy."

## UNIVERSALS

From a study of transformational learning, I developed the *seven universals*. The seven universals were originally developed as an aid to writing transpersonal educational objectives. The similarity to the chakras were not initially evident. As consciousness centers, they represent structures that develop through the intersection of our biological development and the incremental emergence of the soul levels into life. In that sense, the universals are a developmental model that corresponds to Steiner's, Erickson's, and Jean Piaget's developmental theories. As a present time model, a genuinely whole curriculum would have learning objectives that included each universal.

Biologically, we begin at conception as energy and progress through stages of development, each with increasing complexity. The universals are: *energy, experience, relationship, holism, symbol, actualization, transcendence.* While each universal roughly corresponds to a developmental cycle, or life-span stage, we must include all of them as we act toward the child at each stage from conception forward. Healthy development comes from always regarding the individual as whole and complete. For example, *relationship,* as a major category would contain *energy, experience, holism, symbol, actualization,* and *transcendence,*

In the re-education, or process of transformational learning, we begin by awakening our awareness and connection to energy as a soul-force and noetic field. In our teaching, we are responding to the student's soul-actualizing force and aligning the educational experience with that purpose. This can be compared to the "great work"of alchemy. Energy awareness changes the perception through which we access and apply the mystery of each universal.

From the material, organic perspective, we appear to have consciousness as a result of biological development. From a soul perspective, the biological development is a result of spiritual need, which corresponds to Maslow's model. As each stage emerges biologically, our organism has a greater capacity to contain and express our spirit—that is, from the perspective that we are first a spirit being. In classical evolutionary terms, life on the planet develops through

# Consciousness Centers

| CHAKRAS<br>RAMA, BELLENTINE, AJAYA | NEEDS<br>MASLOW | UNIVERSALS<br>WATERMAN |
|---|---|---|
| **PROCREATIVE/ROOT** Survival center; fear of hurting self or others; flight or fight response; seat of paranoia. | **PHYSIOLOGICAL** To survive. | **ENERGY** A metaphor through which we can explore life as a universal form of energy within which we are impelled to move or rest in response to the total lifefield. |
| **SPLEEN** Procreation, species survival, sensuality, sexuality, and creativity. | **SAFETY** To be and feel safe in one's experience and surroundings, free from the potential of harm. | **EXPERIENCE** Life seeks to discover itself, first through sensation. Experience is life engaging itself. |
| **SOLAR PLEXUS** Domination and submission; dynamic and assertive or irritable and angry. | **NURTURE** To be nurtured and cared for and to give caring to others, emotionally and physically. | **RELATIONSHIP** Our first relationship is reflection, then others, deity, and community; begins our concern with power. |
| **HEART** Caring, giving nurture, and mediation of male and female; transforming power. | **BELONGING** To be part of one's surroundings, group, family, community. | **HOLISM** We discover the perspective that unifies the apparent polarization of conflict and the paradox of duality, encompassing unconditionally. |
| **THROAT** We communicate with trust and receptivity while receiving nurturing; traversing abstract, artistic, and unconscious realities. | **ESTEEM** To be seen, recognized, and to feel good about oneself. | **SYMBOL** We use symbolic keys, create abstractly, and journey metaphorically, exploring the unseen consciously. |
| **BROW** The third eye; intuition, self awareness, self-realization, the balance of intellect and emotion, and the integrity of the right-left hand approaches. | **SELF-ACTUALIZATION** To know and fulfill love, to know who one is, and to experience the lived reality of one's potential. | **ACTUALIZATION** We fulfill our destiny and pursue our lifelong transformational learning; mastering our causal relationship to life. |
| **CROWN** Cosmic consciousness, soul awareness, or spiritual illumination. | **TRANSPERSONAL** To experience a connection to higher or spiritual realities; to know one is an integral part of a benevolent universe; using transcendental and spiritual resources to know oneself and master life. | **TRANSCENDENCE** The source of transformation is the transcendent self; personal integration in which our ego joins with a larger, spiritual reality of being human while being divine. |

states in which consciousness evolved from the development of increasingly complex organisms. Human development from conception to maturity appears to recapitulate this evolutionary process. The spiritual view is that consciousness was first and precipitated the evolution of the organism. Comparing this with our brief discussion of Bohm and quantum physics, the explicate order (form) is caused nonlocally from the implicate order (spirit). We will explore this more completely in the next chapter.

# INTEGRATED SYSTEM

We can readily see that there is a relationship between each level of the *three selves, psychosynthesis, chakras,* and *Maslow.* From a psychological perspective, the root, sacral and solar plexus centers are the province of the basic self. The heart, throat and brow are the province of the conscious self. The upper-brow, and crown are the province of the high self. From a spiritual perspective, all of the chakras are in the subtle physical body, and administered by the basic self. Through conscious action and spiritual alliance, we transform these centers and their correspondence in the etheric, or archetypal, body. Huna brings alignment through agreement between the basic, conscious and high self. Psychosynthesis promotes alignment through integration of conflicting forces, and by responding to the call of the Self. In Maslow's hierarchy, alignment occurs through successively meeting the needs from lower to higher. Yoga approaches balancing and aligning the chakras either from drawing the energy up from the base into the brow chakra, or from the crown, through the brow down into the lower chakras.

The range between the root and lower-brow chakra is the personality ego construction. This is the realm of magnetic light, domination and duality. In the magnetic sense, love expresses as a condition. This is the realm in which we work out choice. To guide us in these levels, Buddhism gives us the eight-fold path, yoga gives us the yammas and niyammas, Moses gives us the ten commandments, and Shamanism gives us taboos.

The high self is a type of spiritual entity. It acts through transcendental laws of the spiritual realms. "Beyond the rainbow," so to speak. The high self acts through agreement and invitation. It will not violate our conscious choice or basic self addiction. Injury, such as abandonment and victimization, held in the basic self, are sacrosanct. This, in turn, allows the transforming grace of the high self to engage the process, both on our behalf and on behalf of others.

# INTEGRATIVE TECHNIQUES

In the following integrative techniques, the first two strengthen our connection to the high self. The next two promote manifestation, transformation and healing.

# Journaling

Journaling has a natural flow between the selves. The act of writing provides the vehicle through which the spiritual levels and forms can assist the actualizing flow of our lives. In this case, we will explore a technique for strengthening our relationship between the three selves.

1.  Find a comfortable place to sit where you will not be disturbed. If you like, play some music that makes you feel safe and cared for, at a low volume.

2.  Sit with your writing pad and pen comfortably on your lap.

3.  Ask to be surrounded by the light for the highest good.

4.  Write the word confidential at the top of your journal page. This is to let your basic self know that no one but you will ever know what you write. Journal for a while concerning your *safety, nurture,* and *survival* needs. (It is best not to share this writing with anyone, especially since you told you basic self that it is confidential.)

5.  Close your eyes and imagine that a kind, caring, loving being is standing behind and slightly higher than you are. Feel its presence and caring. Imagine that it puts its hands on your shoulders. This is your high self.

6.  While being careful not to disturb your connection, gently open your eyes and begin to write these words: "Beloved One, concerning your safety, nurture and survival needs I have this to say....." Then continue to write as long as you feel there is inspiration. (You can share what the high self has to say with others, if you choose.)

7.  When you are through, put down your pen, and meditate for awhile.

We are often surprised at the impact of this exercise. The strengthen alignment between the three selves is evident.

As your alignment among your three selves strengthens, you can apply this relationship to healing yourself and others. Remember the high self works in terms of the highest good and will not necessarily give you what you will. When we pray, we focus devotion into the image of what we are praying for. At some point, we release this charged image to God. This is an action between the conscious and basic self. When we release the image to God, we give it to the high self. In the reality of the high self, this energy is amplified ten times and delivered back to accomplish the purpose of the prayer. This is the same process regardless of whether we are praying for wisdom, information, peace, healing, or prosperity. When we "send the light" to others with an intention for health, well being or peace, this energy returns to us tenfold.

1.  Begin with a prayer to be surrounded by the Light for the highest good.

2.  Align inside yourself with the highest consciousness you can imagine, letting go of your thoughts and worries. Empty yourself. When you feel your peace, you are ready to continue.

3.  Focus on the illness or injury. If your focus is a person you are with, it is fine to touch the area of concern. Imagine the outcome you want, i.e., see the person vibrant and well, or see the injury become perfect. Hold this as long as you can while excluding all else, preferably more than 20 minutes. If you see the healing accomplished, you are done, even if it has only been a few minutes.

4.  Let everything go, completely surrendering your image, will, and focus to the high self. If you feel so prompted continue to touch or be attentive to the person.

Remember, your action serves the highest good so trust the response, or lack of response, that you receive. The side benefit of strengthening your three selves alignment may be as, or more, important than what you tried to achieve. Each time you practice, the alignment gets stronger.

Affirmations are a wonderful way to support your actualization and strengthen your three selves alignment. Again, we are using the conscious and basic self to build energy that will be utilized by the high self. I prefer short, condensed affirmations, that combine carefully chosen "I am," action, and "ing" words.

For example:

*I am a whole, sensitive woman, expressing my beauty, sharing my power with love and grace.*

*I am a powerful, sensitive man, sharing my love with honor and affection.*

*I am freely and abundantly receiving large sums of money for my highest good.*

*My body is vibrant, healthy, strong, and free of disease.*

Always ask for the presence of the light for the highest good. When your affirmation is the truth, you will feel it vibrate within you. Repetition is key. As you say it, feel the energy build. Set aside time, or repeat it as you take your daily walk. One technique that can be fun is using one-hundred tooth picks. As you move them from one pile to the next, say your affirmation.

## INNER WORLDS OF CONSCIOUSNESS

Many resources are available that present information, stories and models describing the *spiritual realms,* the *heavens.* Each model reflects the techniques and practices that enable the adherent to access those realities. Simply stated, the *inner worlds* are the human experience of the fabric of creation. As our spiritual awareness develops, we become more conscious of these realities. We form perception that enables us to interact and function in these psychic and spiritual environments.

When we explore common elements in the various models, universals emerge. Some of the universals are that these realities are hierarchical or nested, each having coherent geographies governed by laws and guiding deities. David Bohm's quantum physics suggests that reality is a nested hierarchy in which each reality implicates a higher order reality, all of which are implicated in the one "holomovement." Each realm has a governing spiritual authority that follows the guidance of another higher more universal spiritual authority. These are not authoritarian hierarchies, but rather levels of implicated domains. In the Christian version, a hierarchy of angels administers the "will of God." In the Hindu systems, each hierarchical realm is ruled by a god-head that administers according to a universal plan. We all have experiences in these realities in our sleep. Some of our dreams are actual experiences in spiritual levels. In our dreams, we attend school on these levels or develop prototypes of eventual physical life experiences or manifestation.

My goal is to help you develop practices and concepts that will facilitate your journey in a meaningful way. Conventional wisdom looks at psychological and dream states as artifacts of our physical nature. There is some truth to this. As we have discussed, we organize our perception around our physicality. Just as we project meaning onto our physical surroundings, we also project meaning onto our subtle states. As we resolve our issues with life, deconstruct limiting beliefs, and increasingly organize our thoughts and perceptions from a soul-centered place, we project less, and see through soul or spirit eyes more. Though somewhat idiosyncratic, we see the realities more as they are. The subtle levels interpenetrate the denser ones. So the deepest, or highest, spiritual plane is present. We are also capable of withdrawing our self-awareness into our soul body and transcending as an integrated entity into the higher worlds.

We have a sense of "body" on each level. Each level has a "geography." We shift our awareness to access each level along with its energy and wisdom, or we shift our awareness of self to be conscious on a particular level. The first level is *physical*, including the subtle physical that implicates the meridian and chakra centers. Next is the *astral*. The astral is the imagination. As such, it serves to connect, engage, interface realities and to create patterns and images in the creative process.

These realities ride across each other and interrelate depending on the actions in which we are involved. The *emotional* level is next. In this realm, we are involved with motivation and power. Some systems equate this with causality, calling it the causal realm. This is true to some extent, yet not simply so. Driven by our emotions, we are often reactive, passionate, adversarial, or zealous. This is also a devotional or inspirational level, permeated by the sound of bells. It can be very sweet.

The *mental* level is the source of our ability to create. Beginning with intellectual and rational, the mind is capable of intuition and wisdom. From these realms, we can range from cold rationality to the peace and calm of Buddha. We often see or hear running water at this level, or hear an ohm sound. Edgar Cayce said, "The mind is the builder."

The next realm is known psychologically as the unconscious mind. It is an *etheric*, or *archetypal* reality. In some ways this realm is the blue-print of reality. Everything on this level is symbolic and intentional. Usually, we need some form of symbolic technique to interact with this reality. We are capable of awakening on this level and seeing it directly. This level carries the potential of everything. It almost sounds digital, sounding like a serenade of crickets. This level may appear as a mirror. All reality that has form or structure defining its nature reflects back into the lower worlds. The non-form aspects of spirit and soul, as pure essence, are beyond this mirror. Without a firm sense of self as essence, this level can be very challenging. You may experience it as a void and turn back in fear. You may see it reflect back to you as God, so you believe it and have no sense of moving on to the greater spiritual realities beyond.

Beyond the mirror and the void, is the soul realm. This place is home to us. We are drawn to it by the sense of a flute or conch sound. When we hear this sound inwardly, we a literally called to ourselves as a soul being called to the realm than is native to the soul. We have to turn our sight inward to connect. This direct experience of soul is beyond all the filters of mind, emotion, imagination, and body, yet includes the essence of those expressions.

There are more spiritual realms beyond the soul. I suggest you refer to other readings for a more complete discussion. This is enough to begin stirring our inner awareness. I like references by the *shabd*, or sound current teachers. Books you might refer to are: *Passages Into Spirit*, by John Roger, or books by Sawan Singh, or various writings published by the Sat Biaz press. Your meditation practice will begin to awaken your innate wisdom and attract you to inner and outer schools that are appropriate for your further learning in these areas.

Depth psychology invites us to develop our minds as a perceptive lens that we can use to travel through our internal universe and illuminate its images. From the perspective of energy psychology, we see that the abstract internal universe can now be directly engaged because it exists in a field of energy that fills the space around our physical body.

Our model demonstrates the relationship of the chakras, levels of psychological function, and Maslow's hierarchy. Depth psychology and energy therapy provide a cross-cultural map of consciousness. The psychological functions– such as soul, archetypal, mental, emotional, imaginal, and physical, and Maslow's hierarchy of needs– appear to be universal constructs. The psychological dynamics described by Maslow's needs are contained within the structure of the respective chakras. These centers are a function of the etheric body. The levels of our psychological functioning appear to interact with these centers and act as a field of energy extending to varying degrees around the body. The deeper we move within our center, the farther we extend to the periphery of the aura. The soul is at our center and our periphery. Steiner said that our "soul approaches us from the horizon."

Assagioli's model of the three selves appears consistent with the Huna model and is equally as universal. From an aura balancing perspective, depth models describe a geography of consciousness, which, in turn, reflects interacting fields of life energy. In Huna, the integration and amplification of forces in the basic self are released to the high self producing healing and higher awareness. Psychosynthesis and Huna describe the process of aligning and integrating the human energy fields. These psychologies blend with ancient mysteries to form a coherent model of consciousness, and why should they not if all are differentiated statements of the localization of the whole and are ultimately developed through the lens of human consciousness.

The chakras and Huna represent ancient systems that continue into modern times and emerge in Western psychology with the human potential movement of the 60's that popularized phenomenology and fostered Maslow's psychology of actualization. Assagioli and Jung were stimulated by ancient Eastern perspectives. Ancient Western mysteries emerged through the work of Emerson and Quimby, bridging the creationist teaching of Hildegard of Bingen and the mystical Christianity of Meister Eckhart and inspiring the new thought movement in modern Christianity. We are more powerful when we act truthfully with integrity, impeccability, and congruency. When we do this the movement of our lives and God are the same. The actualizing dimension of our soul fulfills the intention and purpose of our life. Often that purpose is simply to live a joyful life. In the next chapter, we will explore the journey of the soul as a process of the levels of consciousness incarnating as intentional forces into our biological stages of development. This model will set the stage for understanding the function of the time and history in our imperative to understand, evolve, find meaning, and fulfill our nature. Each developmental stage is another foot print, a step forward into the wholeness of self.

## REFERENCES

Assagioli, R. *Psychosynthesis*. New York: Viking Press, 1974.

Judith, J. *Wheels of Life*. St Paul, MN: Llewellyn Publications, 1995.

Maslow, A H. *The Farther Reaches of Human Nature*. New York: Viking Press, 1971.

Myss, C. *Anatomy of the Spirit: The Seven Stages of Power and Healing*. New York: Harmony Books, 1996.

Quimby, P P. *The Quimby Manuscripts*. Edited by H W Dresser. Secaucus, NJ: The Citadel Press, 1969.

Pierrakos, J D. *Core Energetics*. Mendocino, CA: Life Rhythm Publication, 1987.

Reich, W. *Character Analysis*. New York: Simon & Schuster, 1972.

Steiner, R. *Knowledge of the Higher Worlds and Its Attainment*. New York: Anthroposophic Press, 1947.

John-Roger. *Passage Into Spirit*. Los Angeles: Baraka Books, 1984.

# Chapter Four

# JOURNEY OF THE SOUL

We write our origin in mythology, while our time bound, earth centered journey is an epoch story of trial, tribulation, victory, and tragedy. The human spirit prevails, creating meaning, seeking union, and emerging from mysterious alienation into states of grace. The cycle of the myth recapitulates as soon as our soul leaves paradise. We are conceived in paradise, and, in nine months, we encode our destiny into the fabric of our cells. Our bodies recapitulate the natural history of life on earth. At first breath, our body and soul are fused. We are so eager to walk upon this earth that we will risk all to be all.

The fusion of ovum and sperm is a cosmic event. The fate of our eternity is fused with the context of earth and the destiny of human kind. The evolving fetus must receive the incarnation of Holiness. Our challenge is intense. For a time, our only way to communicate is to cry, laugh, gesture, become ill, play, hide, and love. From first breath to puberty, we relive the history of humanity. Each seven years, we pass through an epoch of human existence. As our bodies develop, power grows within us.

Everyone is eager to write upon our mind, heart, and cells the story they have lived and want us to live. Some conspire to shape us in their own image; others know the wisdom of the soul and work with our destiny to draw out and be guided by the teaching that is inherent. The goal is to one day awaken and transform our history into grace and presence, which dissolves the time line into the substance of the soul. For this cause, we walk the earth and place our foot prints on the face of eternity.

## PROCESS OF GOD AND KARMA

Consider that the individual's creative relationship to life may begin prior to conception and engages the physical media of its life at conception. The sperm and ovum become our first creative media. Our bodies remember these early stages of gestation and infancy. Our cells contain the noetic potential to link our soul with the possibilities of the developmental experience. During gestation, our somatic state is highly receptive to the emotional and physical states of our mother and her environment. Someone else chooses the images that go into our psyche for us. As we grow older, we learn the value of discrimination. One aspect of therapy is to transform the images and beliefs that do not work for us. This too may be the agenda of the soul. The final power within all these influences is our own personal destiny. The responsibility for choosing transformation is our own. The fact that we must live and choose lies in the mystery that we are a process of God. We are *holiness* actualizing an individual awareness of universal intelligence and love. Our lover is the universe.

Our parents are our first theology. Their actions and relationship form the psychological symbols representing the father/mother god. This can be congruent or at odds with the innate wisdom of our soul and the universal nature of these symbols as a spiritual and archetypal force. Usually it matches the archetypal bases of our evolution. Like all theology, it can be liberating or dogmatic. At puberty, we internalize the outer relationships. Our path requires us to resolve the parental archetypes as part of our journey.

A central feature of our journey on earth is karma or, in biblical terms, sowing and reaping. Karma is not a negative term. For all practical purposes, it means opportunity. We are responsible for what we do with our lives. Even though we are victimized and legitimately argue that it is not our fault, we nevertheless have a responsibility to respond as the divine essence that we are. When we do, the fault becomes divine blame. When we bring loving to the injury, the karma is healed regardless of how it was brought to our awareness or when it was initiated. Even if we did not cause something that appeared to happen to us, we are responsible for our choices once it happened.

My understanding of karma has been greatly influenced by the teachings of the Shabda Yoga masters. They teach that there are three types of karma: "accrued," "fate," and "reserve." We create accrued karma in the present flow or our lives. Fate karma is an expression of past deeds, choices, attitudes, and omissions from realities prior to this lifetime, which are then structured into the destiny of this lifetime. Reserve karma is the same as fate karma except that it is not necessarily scheduled for this time around. Fate karma, as a function of our destiny, comes into our awareness according to a particular cycle of life or when we have sufficient experience to respond effectively to its potential learning. Reserve karma is like a reserve clause or an option. Once we fulfill the required plan, we can go beyond it and do more.

We live in a field of possibilities. Our involvement has an impact on and is impacted by daily life. Unless we meet daily life with loving, we accrue karma that dulls or limits our capacity to respond. As we learn to live in grace, daily experience is relatively free of accrued karma, fate is transformed, and reserve karma is reevaluated, absolved, or presented in a milder form. At some point, our wisdom exceeds the imbalance and we meet new challenges with relative ease and alignment. We are often, then, in a greater sphere of divine service and service to others. When we are yet to awaken to our wholeness, our safety and the safety of life itself requires that the causes and effects of our lives be limited to the laws of duality. We have the capacity to destroy in the duality-based material worlds. We can transcend into the divine worlds. We cannot destroy in the spiritual worlds. We also have the capacity to bridge the divine and material worlds and have paradise on Earth. Throughout history, grace has been extended to us through anointed ones, or through the direct access of our soul matrix. Salvation is not philosophy or a belief system. It is a psychological transformation that occurs through spiritual means. The saviors of time live within you, awaiting your recognition, then to ignite your soul in the realms of eternity.

As we strengthen ourselves as a soul presence, our spiritual awareness and alignment enable us to remain balanced in the midst of unbalancing realities. The outer energy field of our aura reflects the turmoil and challenges of the day, while the inner or central energy field of our soul space remains balanced. We learn to be in the world but not of it. Whether our path is characterized by fulfilling the cause and effect of the Law of Life or by the action of Grace, we develop and learn through characteristic life cycles.

## THEORIES OF HUMAN DEVELOPMENT

Each theory of human development provides a lens into lifelong learning, which is propelled by our somatic and soul needs. Obstacles and opportunities arise as a teacher of circumstance. These circumstances are course corrections and metaphoric encounters that offer us transformation or new understanding. Life is an actualization process through which each stage represents a classroom in which skills, knowledge, and attitudes pertinent to each stage are drawn forward and developed.

## Eric Erickson

Erickson's developmental theory describes the challenges and choices that we encounter at each stage of our lives. Erickson's view of development begins at birth. At birth, our first breath magnetizes our souls to our bodies for the duration of our physical sojourn.

Each stage presents the individual with choice. Through one's creative response, meaning structures that contain beliefs of a healthy or unhealthy nature are formed. From these choices, we construct positive or negative character structures.

Choice is complex. There are instinctual choices such as breathing or reactions prompted by various kinds of stimulation, and there are volitional choices that are strategies for controlling one's life. Each experience shapes the probability of the next experience and future choice. For example, from birth to two years old we make choices that develop *trust* or *mistrust*. The sense of trust in oneself shapes how we are able to develop *autonomy* in the next stage.

| Erickson's Stages of Development (Galloway) | |
|---|---|
| Age | Character Structures |
| 0 to 2 | **Trust vs Mistrust** Consistency, continuity, genuine regard, and sameness of experience lead to a view of the world as safe and dependable. Inadequate care or inconsistent or negative treatment leads to fear and suspicion. |
| 2 to 4 | **Autonomy vs Doubt** Encouraging the child to try to do what s/he can, at the child's own pace and in the child's own way, leads to autonomy. If too many things are done for the child or if others are too critical or impatient, the child may doubt his/her own ability. |
| 4 to 6 | **Initiative vs Guilt** Giving freedom to initiate activities and careful attention to questions moves the child toward self-initiative. If given rigid, senseless restrictions and a sense of being a nuisance, the child will feel guilty or lack in the face of any self-initiative. |

| Erickson's Stages of Development (Galloway) | |
|---|---|
| **Age** | **Character Structures** |
| 6 to 12 | **Industry vs Inferiority** Recognizing the things the child produces develops a sense of industry. Giving criticism or derision for the child's efforts results in feelings of inferiority. |
| 12 to 19 | **Identity vs Role Confusion** If the youth finds continuity or sameness in his/her personality, especially in the eyes of others in various situations, e.g., work and leisure, then identity develops. If the youth finds instability or discontinuity in his/her perceptions of him/herself in various aspects of life, role confusion results. |
| Young Adult | **Intimacy vs Isolation** Selection of mate and establishment of an occupational pattern lead the young adult to intimacy. Failure in either task leads to a sense of isolation from life and society. |
| Middle Age | **Generativity vs Self-Absorption** The adult who is able to provide the growth potential for the next generation feels a sense of generativity. If the adult is unable to do so, a feeling of self-absorption results. |
| Old Age | **Integrity vs Despair** Being able to accept life as it had to be, results in a sense of integrity. A retrospective view that life was somehow a failure results in despair. |

## John Dewey and Jean Piaget

John Dewey, though he did not focus on particular stages, did share a similar viewpoint with Steiner, Erickson, and Piaget concerning the process of learning. They all believed that the guiding principle of education was character development through an appropriately sequenced, experiential curriculum, and that the connection of the teacher and the student provided an essential and vital element of the learning experience. Dewey was concerned that  information not be taught separate from experience.

As we survey Piaget's developmental theory, we discover that each stage is more appropriate for some types of experience than others. Consequently, there is a pacing, or congruence, between the developmental cycle, and the type of learning that is appropriate.

Though they each speak to different audiences, they each developed what I call a soul-centered approach.

## Piaget's Stages of Development (Galloway)

| Age | Stage | Description |
|---|---|---|
| 0 to 2 | Sensorimotor | Learning tied to immediate experience; external actions on physical things and events; behavior is egocentric. |
| 2 to 7 | Pre-Operational | Use of language becomes important; learner is no longer bound to an immediate sensory environment; insights are intuitive; learning is imitative. |
| 7 to 11 | Concrete Operational | Thought is concrete and literal; person understands functional relationships; reason is logical and reversible. |
| 11 on | Formal Operational | Thought is logical, rational, and abstract; person can reason on the basis of hypothetical statement. |

*Joseph Chilton Pearce*

Pearce, in *Evolution's End,* discusses the emergent nature of learning. The innate potential of each stage—whether physical, imaginal, emotional, mental, archetypal, or spiritual—is activated by environmental encounters. Extrapolating from Piaget's stages of intellectual development, Pearce makes the case that the least understood and most neglected of these potentials occurs at puberty and during the mid-teens. These last two cycles awaken the individual to abilities and to resources of a spiritual nature. Being secure in oneself as a soul, experiencing oneself as an active participant in a universal consciousness, and responding to the environment in ecologically healthy ways are expressions of the effective engagement of the teenage passages. Pearce believes that actual health and intelligence increase when the educational challenges meet the potential for development of this stage. At puberty, nature invites us to perpetuate the accustomed historical patterns of humanity or to make history our springboard into the creation of a more soul-centered civilization. According to Pearce, the spiritual and intellectual potential of the teenage stages, if unengaged, lingers into adult life, awaiting the

68

initiatory encounter. For these reasons, Pearce suggested an extension of Piaget's model to include "First Post Operational" and a "Second Post Operational" stages of intellectual development. I call these the *noetic stages*, which will be explored later. Aurobindo might call them *supramental stages*.

In keeping with Pearce's theory, when I was thirteen, I began to experience a presence that provided deeper insights into the mystical meaning of the Scriptures. These insights met with opposition from my Sunday school teacher, who wanted me to learn the dogma. My soul wanted to awaken to the experience of Spirit. By nineteen, I had my first illuminating experience of spiritual realities.

I was reminded of my teenage thirst for spirituality when I traveled in France in the summer of 1996. We visited Taize, France. Thousands of teenagers from all over Europe were gathered for the simple and powerful approach to spirituality that was offered there. Brother Rogers, the founder, began his ministry toward the end of World War II. Over the years, he developed a simple approach to spirituality. The only theology appears to be that of the "risen Christ." He developed a form of singing worship. No preaching. No dogma. Simple singing together of one's relationship to the Divine. In some ways, it reminded me of Gregorian chants, the Hindu practice of singing bhajans, the universal practices of chanting together, or the Native American singing practices. Brother Rogers developed many of the songs. The songs appear to weave the participant into a fabric with the Holy Spirit. Singing together is the only form of worship.

His approach is especially appealing to young people. They come to Taize and learn to sing, work, and play together. The worship engenders an experience of spiritual connection. The flow of spirit may surface a need to talk about one's concerns and problems, to which counselors listen. From this perspective, the singing is a spiritual practice from which continuing spiritual pursuits and experiences evolve.

On the shadow side, teenage behavior that pushes the limits of life through drug abuse, suicide, and drive-by shootings are examples of this developmental stage. Depression is a symptom of encountering the immensity of one's consciousness without adequate character development. Looking for heroes to engage one's spirituality is developmentally sensitive in the teen years, positive or negative. The teenager is at risk when the developmental experience does not provide adequate foundation for transcendental encounters, when the needed guide through the dark night of the soul is unavailable, or when bonding with the guide is not secure. The guide must be able to incarnate the consciousness for which the teenager is ready. Consistency, example, respect, boundaries, joy, and love are essential.

Hillman, in his process of *soul making*, describes how human development is driven by an archetypal destiny and is not a result of the developmental experience. According to Hillman in his "acorn theory" of human development, the adult, as destiny, is alive in the child. Developmental perspectives, per se, are a vehicle through which we actualize our destiny. Personally, I do not see much difference in these two approaches. Each approach is a form of educare', or *drawing out*.

## Rudolf Steiner

Like Erickson, Steiner believed that balance and appropriate developmental experience are essential for healthy character development. For Steiner, each stage contains distinct qualities that require respect, even sacred regard, for healthy development. For example, if we learn to read before our change of teeth, we are forced to use energy that would have gone to *will* development. In other words, learning to read too early may weaken our will. Each stage contains its own nature and purpose. When a child is forced to learn in one cycle in ways more appropriate to a future cycle, the future is robbed for the sake of more rapid progress in the present. In other words, if a child is forced to grow up too soon or to participate in adult desires, the child's future is robbed in order to pay for the trauma or competing interests of the present. This results in a character development that is prone to assimilate too much negative energy from the environment. The child's response to experience, and the types of experiences that are presented, healthy or unhealthy, cause energy to be taken into the physical and psychic constitution. If this energy is *negative,* it may block spiritual expression.

Each stage in Steiner's system lasts seven years. Each biological stage provides the framework into which the respective levels of the soul incarnate and express through the body. For example, at birth the first breath connects the body and the unconscious mind or archetypal soul. Birth through seven is the biological time when the *will* is developing. As the *will* develops organically, the unconscious becomes more expressive through the physical life of the child. *Will* corresponds to Erickson's first three stages. When the physical and psychological levels are not in sync, the spiritual expression may be distorted.

While developing the Passages of the Soul's Journey, I drew upon Steiner's work, anthroposophical writers, and my own experience. Steiner saw the psycho-biological development as a receptacle for the incarnating qualities of the soul.

Steiner believed our life experience begins at conception. In a sense, our bodies, prior to birth, review the evolution of life and then review human history through the developmental cycles. Steiner divides the nine months of gestation into trimesters, believing that each trimester reflects a foundation for future states of development. This raises the possibility that, besides the mother's experience during gestation, the cell memory contains reflections of the wisdom of life itself.

| Passages of the Soul's Journey (Steiner, O'Neal, Treichler) | | |
|---|---|---|
| **Age** | **Stage** | **Passages** |
| Intention to Conception | | Our lifetime begins with the consideration of how best to weave our experience, nature, and potential into an effective destiny. We are passed the stage when any life will do and look forward to greater spiritual awakening and fulfillment of our dreams. Our destiny is formulated through a divine collaboration. Time, place, parents, and circumstances are matched to our capacity to pursue our heart's desire. |
| Conception to Birth | | The moment and circumstances of our conception are important. The contact of our soul selectively fuses the genetic mix that sets the creation of our physical body into motion. Each trimester reviews the potential foundation for the coming life. The development of the fetus recapitulates each stage of natural and human history. We incorporate this experience as cell memory in support of our physical survival and somatic wisdom. The physical, mental, and emotional states of the mother and her relationships affect this process. |

| Passages of the Soul's Journey (Steiner, O'Neal, Treichler) | | |
|---|---|---|
| Age | Stage | Passages |
| Birth to 7 | Will and Archetypal | Our incarnating soul transforms the prototype body into its own. Physical, emotional, and organic learning occurs through imitation. Healthy will develops through physical action, emotional expression, and environmental response. Perception is archetypal. |
| 7 to 14 | Feeling and Imaginal | Concepts and the soul and spirit organs develop. The powers of thought emerge. The feeling, sentient nature becomes the vehicle for the imaginal and creative soul to assert its expression and development. Learning is through inspiration and fantasy. Learning capacity and memory develop. Character develops through the emulation of loving authority. Child may alternate between sympathy and antipathy, pleasure and pain, fear and courage. Hypersensitivity or less sensitivity or dullness may occur. At about 9, the future is anticipated, stirring a beginning impulse for individuation. |
| 14 to 21 | Thinking and Emotional | Inner duality is awakened and asserted through defining self and separating from parents. Abstract conceptual thinking emerges. The focus, discipline, and experience of thinking provide structure and expression for emotion as passion, enthusiasm, and causal soul. Karma calls. The power of love, sexuality, and creativity awaken more fully in the body. The force of love begins to mature, balancing extremes of passion and compassion through the intimacy of the feeling soul. Body completes its maturity. At around 15, this stage is balanced through the awakening call to one's inherent goodness through kinship with life. At around 18, holiness as a divine expression awakens. |

| Passages of the Soul's Journey (Steiner, O'Neal, Treichler) | | |
|---|---|---|
| Age | Stage | Passages |
| 21 to 28 | Doing and Mental | Activity in the world becomes the vehicle for the mental soul as an expression of intelligence through creativity. Memory and articulation of one's perspective are heightened. Buoyancy, vigor, and sociability characterize life. One is compelled to experience. It is a good time to complete one's formal education. |
| 28 to 35 | Synthesis/ Reflection and Intuitive | Reflection on and synthesis of one's life provide the vehicle for intuition or an intimacy with spiritual intelligence. The world comes into focus along with the questioning of meaning. The urge to complete old projects and education is accompanied by an expanded sense of self. A passion to be right can make one prone to pontificating, correcting others, and asserting one's self-righteousness void of warmth. Balance occurs through turning inward the tendency for analysis and dispassionate diagnosis to addressing one's own weaknesses. Charity toward and appreciation of others provides balance and healthy perspective. |
| 35 to 42 | Mastery and Awakening | The synthesis, reflection, and completion of the previous stage bring mastery. Mastery in living provides the context for a greater awakening to the soul realms. One may experience a dark night of the soul. Identifying oneself through the mirror of outer notoriety and perspectives of others gives way to acknowledging one's inherent worth. We are fully incarnated, less propelled by circumstances, and act more from inner motivation. One achieves psychological maturity. |
| 42 to 49 | Clarity and Mani-festation | Clarity of mind, vision, and executive action provide a vehicle for greater manifestation in life. Productivity, innovation, imagination, and a spiritual vigor typify this stage. Careers may be reshaped. One's personal life impacts others more forcefully. |

| Passages of the Soul's Journey (Steiner, O'Neal, Treichler) | | |
|---|---|---|
| **Age** | **Stage** | **Passages** |
| 49 to 56 | Intentional-ity and Realization | Intention forms the conduit through which one's action in the world brings the realization of ideas and soulness. External confrontation is often resolved through a greater depth of self or soul realization. A native strength and ability to fulfill one's ideas as intention in their final form emerge. Ability to change and adapt are important. Trauma and transformation are a sign of the times. Avoidance of self-knowledge may weaken the heart while bodily forces move from being generative to a spiritual power. The opportunity exists to promote new causes through the force of wisdom and maturity even beyond one's latent skills. Wisdom can permeate one's whole being. New life elements can radiate, or one can become dominating and irascible. |
| 56 to 63 | Leadership and Service | A consciousness of leadership emerges. This leadership is selfless and is a spiritual channel for divine service. Almost magically, one's ideas motivate and inspire others. One's maturity elicits devoted help and brings out the latent force in others to unify and heal communities. The immature person lacks this special power and is inept except, perhaps, within their own limited, narrow groups. |
| 63 to 70 | Elder/Crone and Wisdom | One is fully born as an expression of the Divine. One is genuinely human. As an elder or crone, a source of wisdom permeates one's expression and the fruits of a life's work can be shared through things of genuine interest to the world. For one who has failed in the preparation of spiritual independence, these are times of spiritual poverty. |

| Passages of the Soul's Journey (Steiner, O'Neal, Treichler) | | |
|---|---|---|
| **Age** | **Stage** | **Passages** |
| 70 to Death | Revolution and Consumation | These may be more inward times. One has the opportunity to free oneself from the opinion and restraints of one's own accomplishments and range free in spirit. Even a misspent life can break free at this time. Liberated from any social conscience, anything is a possibility to the free spirit. Senility for some may be an outer appearance, while the spirit arranges the inner worlds. |

## JOURNEY OF THE SOUL MODEL

Steiner offers us deeper understanding of the developmental experience. Our incarnation is a continuing process. The foundation that began at conception and continues through adulthood interweaves our evolutionary experience as a soul, as a genetic species, and our potential as a divine being. Steiner's therapies and educational methods are based on this deep understanding of the soul's journey. Steiner sought to educate in ways that integrated the flow of energy in and between the various dimensions of self and life.

Life as art, movement, and expression are major aspects of this learning. Education is also therapy. By awakening and reintegrating the natural rhythms and flow of consciousness, limitations are transformed. To help an autistic child, Steiner developed what he called Eurythmy as a system of archetypal movement. The autism was transformed, and the child grew up to be a medical doctor.

Anthroposophy continues to explore and refine Steiner's work. In my growth and development, I experienced dramatic changes when I walked into a new phase or resolved some aspect of my life. Phenomenally, my experience was one of a greater beingness awakening within myself. At times, I felt like a deeper level of my soul incarnated. I observed my clients and students having similar experiences.

I was tutoring a university student who had been admitted through a special program. She was having difficulty passing basic English, ostensibly because she came from a substandard high school. Rather than teach her the mechanics of English, I assumed she either knew them or would gain them quickly if she could awaken to the inherent life of language and the natural antecedents of grammar within her humanity. The breakthrough came when I was attempting to bring her into an organic understanding of the grammatical syntax of a simple essay. I had her tell me a story of a familiar event. In this case, it was an evening out with her friends. She began with a time when they met, continued with the main episodes of the evening, and ended with their reflections before they went their respective ways. She made the connection, which triggered her into another story. I don't recall the content, but this time she became so immersed in the story that she lost her self-consciousness, stood on a chair, and spoke as if addressing a large audience with complete abandon. When she was done, I told her to go take her basic English test. She passed and went on to become an honors scholar in Shakespearean literature and drama. When I last saw her she was on her way to England on a summer Shakespearean scholarship.

## Journey of the Soul Chart

The following chart combines the theories of Steiner, Erickson, Piaget and Pearce. Steiner inspired the time-line concept. A combination of spiritual and psychological models inspired the levels of consciousness. Erickson and Piaget provide a way to interface with the various developmental theories. The outline of Piaget's stages includes two additional stages proposed by Pearce. To create the model, I combined material from Steiner, anthroposophy, and my own experience.

I adopted Steiner's concept of human development and, with the inclusion of observations from current anthroposophists, created the model presented in the journey of the soul chart (which elaborates on the developmental stages), and the chart that compares the developmental models in the context of the incarnating soul qualities throughout the life span. For example, from birth to seven the interacting biological, psychological, and environmental forces develop one's *will*. The *will* is the vehicle for the life pattern or the intentionality of the archetypal structure of one's destiny. We might say that the *will* is the agency of noesis. Then, developing our *feeling* nature becomes the vehicle for imagination. If the feelings become blocked, the imagination is impaired.

The time line (age) begins at conception and ends at death. The left side represents the functional and structural progression of our development. The right side represents the incarnating self, as aspects

## JOURNEY OF THE SOUL COMPARATIVE MODELS

| PIAGET PEARCE | ERICKSON | STEINER WATERMAN | AGE | SOUL |
|---|---|---|---|---|
| | | GESTATION | -9 mo | INTENTION |
| SENSORI-MOTOR PRE-OPERA-TIONAL | TRUST V. MISTRUST AUTONOMY V. DOUBT INITIATIVE V. GUILT | WILL | 0 | ARCHETYPAL |
| CONCRETE OPERATIONAL | INDUSTRY V. INFERIORITY | FEELING | 7 | IMAGINAL |
| FORMAL OPERATIONAL | IDENTITY V. ROLE CONFUSION | THINKING | 14 | EMOTIONAL |
| PEARCE: | INTIMACY V. ISOLATION | DOING | 21 | MENTAL |
| 13 - 14 FIRST POST OPERA-TIONAL | | SYNTHESIS REFLECTION | 27 | INTUITIVE |
| (LOCALITY TO NON-LOCALITY) | GENERATIVE V. SELF ABSORPTION | MASTERY | 35 | AWAKENING |
| 14 ONWARD SECOND POST OPERATIONAL | | CLARITY | 42 | MANIFESTATION |
| (BEYOND ALL DYNAMICS) | | INTENTIONALITY | 49 | REALIZATION |
| | | LEADERSHIP | 56 | SERVICE |
| | INTEGRITY V. DESPAIR | ELDER/CRONE | 63 | WISDOM |
| | | REVOLUTION | 70 | CONSUMATION |

LIFE EXPERIENCE WITHDRAWS FROM THE BODY AT DEATH, AND TRANSFERS INTO SOUL MATRIX

of the Soul. Functionally, the ego develops as a way to interact effectively with experience. The functional ego instinctually develops with the biological process. The structured part of the ego develops through our interaction with others and through reflection on our experience. Steiner believed that the quality of one's experience predisposes one to take in positive or negative life force from the physical, psychic, and spiritual environments. When development occurs in balance with the cycle, optimum conditions exist for the

incarnating soul or soul aspect.

Causality in this model combines the *synchronistic, linear*, and *emergent* mechanisms described by Jung. The time line is *linear* cause and effect. "A" causing "B" is observable in time. Within the time line, cycles of development occur that are *emergent*. The linear development sets the stage for an emergent development in which the next cycle incubates in the previous one. The seed of the next cycle incubates within the structure of its preceding stage. To some extent, the emergent and linear causalities can be explained consciously and rationally. The causality of the incarnating soul aspect is *synchronistic*. Synchronistic refers to the bolts out of the blue and meaningful coincidences. The effects in the temporal experience are caused from a transcendental source. The soul unfolds the local dimensions of the personality and organism through the time line from the nonlocal reality of the spiritual worlds. The rational mind can observe and describe synchronistic effects and even evaluate them once their possibility is accepted. From a Jungian perspective, synchronicity is essential for accounting for archetypal influences in the psyche. Our time-bound life presents opportunities to incorporate transcendental aspects of ourselves into our conscious expression.

Referring to the chart, psycho-biological development is essentially a receptacle for the incarnating consciousness. Each cycle represents the natural opportunities one has. Consequently, if each stage progresses in a healthy manner, a full range of consciousness is developed. Each stage has all that we need to gain the development of that stage. Natural gifts and potentials within the soul are often blocked by poor nutrition or poor emotional support, pressure to learn too quickly, adversarial teaching methods, or trauma. Essentially, the experiences, choices, and developing constitution of the individual draws out and makes conscious, the deeper levels of the personality. Said another way, each developmental stage provides a context for deeper levels of expression from within the individual.

As the psychobiological development is capable of containing and expressing a greater aspect of our being, that greater aspect enters into the time line. Organic and psychological structures are the constructed context for the aspects of the soul to incarnate into physical life. The physical, emotional, and mental health of the ego or *time-line self* are essential for healthy soul movement. Each stage is a sacred opportunity to connect the soul with the learning experience. The learning experience is an offering to the soul. The root meaning of education is to "draw out." This relationship of organic development, psychological balance, and appropriate learning experience is the key to the harmonious development of one's soul life and life mastery. In the chart, the soul's movement through the matrix of personality and the life span flows from top to bottom and from right to left.

## Journey Into Time

We have lived before. Our awareness of self extends into far distant realities. Our eternity becomes a foot print on this time line, in this place. All is revealed through the portal of now.

- Take a deep breath and relax. Bring your awareness into your body, caressing each cell with awareness and love. Be aware of the space around your physical body. Feel your love surrounding and permeating your physical body.

- Focus your awareness into the center of your head, seeing a light grow from that point into a sphere of light. See your self inside of that sphere.

- Imagine that you are traveling back in time to your conception. Extend to an awareness prior to your conception. Sense your eternity and your journey prior to this incarnation.

- Sense the awareness of your parents and your essence at the moment of conception. Infuse the moment of your conception with Divine Love. Become aware of you as your developing fetus. Sense the recapitulation of all life forms from one cell, through reptilian, four legged and two legged beings.

- Go now to your birth. See the physical and metaphysical reality join. Progress through each developmental cycle. As your biological self emerges, feel the incarnation of that aspect of your soul consciousness. Progress through each developmental cycle to the present time.

- Take a moment to relax into this field of consciousness, appreciating all that you are.

The awe that comes with the miracle of birth is a catalyst to understanding the incarnation of the human soul. The dimension of time enables us to master cause, effect, and the creative mission of our actualization. We learn to master protocol through the textured richness of life. In the alchemical reagent of our personal psyche, a second miracle occurs. We enfold the developmental time-line into the eternal present of our own space. We become increasingly more like a presence of God. We enfold the events, choices and works-in-progress into the implicate order of our *sphere of influence.* Once enfolded, we can rework the material in a world-of-our-own-making, a world of our own possibility.

In the next chapter, in order to bring this understanding into our personal sphere, I enfold the models of consciousness and journey of the soul into an applied spiritual psychology. I call this model *noetic psychology.* In this endeavor, I invite you to use the chapter to further embrace your perception and to practice the protocols that, through the power of your own space, will assist you to transform your relationship to self, holiness, the universe, God and time. Remember, the foot print is evidence that your eternity incarnated and made an expression on the surface of life. You are the effect and the cause, the alpha and the omega. When you lift your foot you take that impression with you, as yourself.

## REFERENCES

Erickson, E H. *Childhood and Society.* New York: Norton Press, 1963.

Galloway, C. *Psychology of Learning and Teaching.* St. Louis, MO: McGraw-Hill, 1976.

Hillman, J. *The Soul's Code.* New York: Random House, 1996.

Jung, C G. *On the Nature of the Psyche.* New York: Bollingen Foundation, 1960.

O'Neal, G and G. *The Human Life.* Spring Valley, NY: Mercury Press, 1992.

Pearce, J C. *Evolution's End.* San Francisco, CA: Harper, 1992.

Piaget, J, and B Inhelder. *Psychology of the Child.* Scranton, PA: Harper San Francisco, 1991.

Steiner, R. *Education as an Art.* New York: Anthroposophic Press, 1970.

Sing, S. *Philosophy of the Masters.* India: Radhaswami, 1973.

Treichler R. *Soulways.* Stroud, England: Hawthorn, 1969.

# Chapter Five

# NOETIC PSYCHOLOGY

Noetic Psychology is a synthesis of universal themes that weave through ancient mysteries, modern psychological, and therapeutic practices to produce a simple and powerful approach. It requires trust in our natural humanity, and the disciplined conversion of our mind into its spiritual form. Therapeutic issues are dualistic, even adversarial. They are conflicting and divisive constructs that reflect as distortions in the noetic field. They are *reversals* of positive intensional aims, that, ironically, function to awaken our soul nature. In Noetic Field Therapy, the unconscious dimensions of the issue become visible as patterns in the noetic field. In order to understand the simplicity of NFT, we will first explore its complexity. The first step is to deepen our understanding of the relationship of energy, consciousness, and symbolic activity.

## THERAPEUTIC MODELS

The therapeutic process is a specific application of our life process. Life is always working with us to resolve difficulties. It works from within us and through events reflected back to us. Consciousness always unfolds according to where we are in ourselves. We are the starting point and the ending point. We are the personal experience of the alpha and omega. How we structure our reality and what we are focusing on is the reference point for the present reality. We navigate consciousness from where we are. This is the power of now. When we grasp the therapeutic process, the transformation unfolds through universal procedures, uniquely styled by our choices and creations. When our purpose is congruent through mind, body, and soul, we are in health. When it is not congruent, we are out of balance.

Most therapeutic models proceed from a phenomenological orientation. Shared themes emerge that are common to the ancient mysteries and modern therapies. Common themes are: actualization of a core source of health, deconstruction of limiting beliefs, and affirmation of the premise that life is self healing. I chose three therapies that reflect universal themes common to phenomenology and NFT. Therapies that are thematically related to NFT also reflect the prototype of Husserlian reduction. These therapies are: Rogerian Therapy, Experiential Focus Therapy, and Thought Field Therapy (TFT). From the NFT perspective, these therapies are effective because they help clients shift their self-definition from externally oriented constructions of self to an experience of self as soul-centered. In the process, the client accesses an inherent transformational resource that is powerful, loving, intelligent, and divine. Rogerian therapy emphasizes the power of the therapist's presence and alignment with a higher principle. Experiential focus therapy demonstrates the power of focus on the felt sense to access the belief structure and the value of the client's awareness as a means to index transformation and the felt shift as a spiritual expression. TFT helps us understand the transformative power of protocol as an intrinsic dynamic of the noetic field. In Thought Field Therapy, deconstruction occurs by tapping points on the meridians.

In NFT, we guide the client and promote a distinct awareness of the elements of the experience that formed or are forming the problem. I use *client* in a metaphoric way. In self-therapy, you are your own helper and helpee. With a friend, you are a co-client. We isolate the emotion or feeling. Was the client feeling pain, torture, rage, fright, lust, delight, or victimization? What thoughts did the client have in response to the event? Did the client decide s/he was shameful, guilty, defective, bad? What actions occurred? Who did what to whom? What were the circumstances in which this occurred? As we pursue and clarify these distinctions, the bonds holding together the elements of the cathexes, blocks, or perturbations are loosened, or "reduced." By following this procedure, we are applying the Husserelian protocol. When we insert a belief into our psychological persona, *thinking, feeling* and *doing* are bound and predisposed to occur in a specific way, consistent with the parameters of the belief. Our psyche is "trapped," so to speak. *Thinking, feeling,* and *doing* are referred to as the *three fires*. The unraveling of the three fires is what Husserl called "deconstruction." This action frees the spirit to move through that area of consciousness, and the intentionality of the soul reemerges as a directional entity. This is, also, the experience of epiphany or transformation.

## Unconditional Positive Reduction

Issues often begin with early experiences in which we try to share our loving, express our excitement, or try to get something we need. When those early events are met with control, or a manipulative agenda, in exchange for the loving we want, the acknowledgment we need, or the basic needs we require—let alone a violent or indifferent response—we adapt by developing distorted beliefs concerning love, need, and empowerment.

Phenomenological reduction can be a simple therapeutic process. For example, Carl Rogers developed "unconditional positive regard" as a therapeutic tool. The basic technique is simple. As clients articulate their beliefs and conclusions concerning their issue, the therapist witnesses with *unconditional positive regard*. The client talks, and the therapist loves them without judgment. This is a reductive process. An issue can only form when the client's early action received a response of indifference, aggression or manipulation.

Issues originate from experiences in which the client is coerced or manipulated through their needs to believe that they have to be what others want them to be in order to get safety, shelter, or nurture. These beliefs require manipulative or agenda-laden responses in order to maintain their inertia. When the client articulates the resulting issue or trauma and is met with loving or unconditional positive regard, the sedimenting belief system begins to deconstruct. The "glue" that holds the issue together requires an adversarial or manipulative response in order to maintain its cohesion.

Conversations between injured, controlling, or protective agendas tends to perpetuate a negative self-regard. Our beliefs need reinforcement to persist. The presence of loving, acceptance, and the absence of manipulation disperses the negative self-regard. The unconditional loving deconstructs the negative belief. At some point, the client's intentionality for love, recognition, or support reasserts itself into the flow of the therapeutic relationship and the noesis emerges as the experiential correlation of the issue, as a healing epiphany.

## Experiential Focus Therapy

In her book, *Integrating Spirituality in Counseling*, Elfie Hinterkopf discusses the "felt shift" of experiential focus therapy, developed by Eugene Gendlin, as a form of spiritual assertion. The client is guided to focus on the "felt sense" (noema) that corresponds to the presenting issue. By following the felt sense, the client further attunes to the energy field of that issue and is invited to elaborate. The reduction occurs while the client focuses on the felt sense and elaborates on the images that present themselves.

In NFT, the practice of focusing on one's subjective experience is an effective means to assist clients to open and deepen awareness and to access their therapeutic resources. The therapist assists the client to focus and elaborate while being present with an intention of unconditional acceptance. The context created by drawing out the client in this way is deconstructing and is sufficient for the felt shift (noesis) to emerge. The subjective assessment of the felt sense and felt shift help the client to mentally track their psychological movement and change. When transformation occurs, the client experiences a felt shift. The felt shift is a spiritual assertion of the experiential correlation of the intentionality (noesis) and its sedimented beliefs.

## Thought Field Therapy

Roger J. Callahan developed TFT by relating his study of applied kinesiology to his therapeutic work with clients who were expressing phobias. He discovered that the acupuncture points along the meridians are an integral part of the construction and anchoring of memory and emotion (sedimentation). He calls the negative emotion that is distorting the thought field a "perturbation" (noema).

For typical conditions, Callahan developed basic algorithms or recipes for treatment. Algorithms are tapping sequences based on specific symptoms. For more complex cases, diagnosis using applied kinesiology is necessary. To track the transformational process, clients are guided to rate their distress on a scale of one to ten, one being no distress and ten being the maximum distress. He calls this rating a SUDs level (subjective units of distress).

In the therapeutic protocol, the client attunes to the perturbation in the thought field while tapping the acupuncture points in specified sequences (deconstruction). According to Callahan, this procedure results in cure or transformation (noesis) of the symptom (noema). TFT-tapping unblocks the flow of energy in the meridian and by doing so releases the perturbation or distortion in the thought field. The client reports "subjective units of distress (SUDs)" levels to evaluate the transformation. Cure occurs when the client is free of the harassing negative emotion or perturbation while attuning to the images that represent the distressing situation.

When applying TFT, clients first attune to the perturbation (P) in their thought field (TF).

*[Briefly] ... a perturbation is a proposed entity in the thought field. The P is viewed as the fundamental and basic cause of all negative emotions . . . and . . . correlates with specific energy points on the body. Successful therapy subsumes or reduces the impact of the Ps in the thought field. . . . A P is a subtle, but clearly isolable aspect of a thought field which is responsible for triggering all negative emotions. (p 121, Callahan).*

The TF is fundamental to TFT.

*The dynamic and limitless potentiality of the thought field is what makes TFT a psychological treatment. When one is trained to diagnose TFs, it becomes immediately apparent that the structure of the TF creates dynamism in the individual. . . . When the relevant TF is attuned, it brings to the fore the specific P's and related information which are active in a problem and vital to understanding what is called for in the treatment situation. (p 126, Callahan).*

According to Callahan, "The (regular) dictionary defines field as 'a complex of forces that serve as causative agents in human behavior.' More generally, a field is an invisible nonmaterial structure in space which has an effect upon matter."

Simplified, the technique proceeds as follows:

1.    The therapist determines what algorithms to use by talking to the client.

2.    The client attunes to the perturbation in the thought field and is asked for a SUDs level.

3.    The therapist guides the client in the relevant self-tapping sequence while the client focuses on the perturbation.

4.    The client is asked for another SUDs level.

5.    The therapist assesses the effectiveness of the treatment and pursues ancillary treatment or direction.

The result of this approach is often rapid and effective. I was introduced to TFT through Suzanne Connelly Workshops, 70 Payne Place 6, Sedona, AZ 86336; 1 (800) 656-4496.

## SELF AS ENERGY

In our discussion of Rogerian Therapy, Experiential Focus Therapy, and TFT, I invited you to explore the reductive prototype embedded in these approaches and to further explore the nature of NFT. This section takes a further look at the intentional nature of psychic energy, the dynamics of balancing blockages, and the healthy expression and actualization of that energy. First, we will explore the somatic and psychodynamic behavior of psychic and spiritual energy. Then, we will explore the application of therapy through the energy qualities in the Noetic Field surrounding the body and explore the psychological structure as an energy form.

### Somatic Energy Balancing

The relationship between symbolic (meaning) structures and the movement or balance of energy in the psyche has a long history. Freud postulated that the healthy "cathexis" (build-up) of "libido" (psychic energy) is "directionally fulfilling" (intentional). When blocked through anticathexis, psychological problems result. "Psychoanalysis" deconstructs the complexes and returns the client to health. Reich also recognized that psychological imbalance occurs when the flow of "orgone" (psychic energy) becomes blocked. The "armoring" (blocked energy) accumulates in the related part of the body. Treatment focuses on deconstructing the body armoring. I find the similarity of Riech's map of the armoring and the Chakra system of Eastern yogic psychology striking. It impresses me that similar maps of psychic energy can be developed through two heuristic events so far apart in distance and time.

Like the liberated chi in TFT and the movement of the felt sense in experiential focus therapy, libido, and orgone are intentional somatic energies. The flow of chi is channeled by the meridians of the body. Libido arises from the instinctual, physical drives that become mental and emotional complexes when sublimated. It is simply life force, which serves to fulfill the inscriptions of life. Whereas, TFT accesses the complex through attunement and directly treats the energy structure. Freud accessed the thought field through more passive techniques, such as "free association." Reich, as well, focused on the body armoring, though he realized that orgone, in some cases, could stream outside the body and could be balanced by replenishing it from a surrounding cosmic field. Reich is supported in his assertion by the apparent existence of chi and prana recognized by their respective cultures as a source of dynamic energy resident in the physical space that surrounds us, which can be used to replenish the body and enhance psychological health by using techniques that bridge the body to the implicate and transcendental energy sources through consciousness.

## THE CALL

Jung also viewed psychic energy as actualizing and directional. Embedded within this psychic movement are symbolic and archetypal structures that determine the circulation, flow, or containment of the energy. We organize our beliefs in symbolic complexes. As these complexes are deconstructed in the therapeutic process, the gravitational flow of the psychic energy carries us into our center, our soul-space.

A similar dynamic is expressed in the psychology of Maslow. The intentional flow of these energies is the result of an inherent hierarchy of needs, similar in function and structure to the chakras. As the issue relating to these needs resolves, we experience the fulfillment of these needs as transcendence or actualization.

Assagioli understood the therapeutic significance of the gravitational call of the "high self" or soul. We adapt to the level of functioning that meets our needs and that appears to provide effective solutions. External forces can disrupt this adaptation. The call of the high self can also disrupt our equilibrium. *Call* means that a sense of our soul unfolds into our normal ego-centered awareness. This may begin as a feeling of "home sickness" that does not seem to fit an external place. Our response to this call acts as a deconstructing influence on our limiting beliefs and ego-centered self concept. We experience Pearce's post-operational stages as a *call*.

Many of Jung's and Assagioli's therapeutic protocols call for the synthesis of opposites. The synthesis of the oppositional forces awakens us in deeper, or higher levels, progressively shifting our identity from our ego to our soul.

## TRANSOMATIC FRONTIERS

The theories and practices of Freud, Jung, Reich, Maslow, Assagioli, Callahan, Gendlin, and Husserl describe transformation as the deconstruction of symbolic structures, or complexes, as a means to free the healthy intentional aims of psychic, or *soul* energy. As a result, a more energized, expansive, integrated, insightful, centered, and transcendental state occurs. Our custom is to attribute these energies to some intrinsic somatic structure such as a symbolically coded engram contained biochemically in specialized tissue. Allegedly, this code is then retrieved cognitively and appears in our perception as an abstraction. "Cell memory" is a useful therapeutic construct and appears to actually exist. We also appear to have consciousness independent of our bodies, that appears to precede and survive the life of our body. Yet, rarely do we consider that when we metaphorically speak of energy and the field nature of consciousness that there is an actual transomatic and tangible field of energy that extends the range of "self" beyond the physical body. When we do embrace this viewpoint, often we stop with the concept and do not continue into the therapeutic implications. We generally stop with the assumption that it has no practical therapeutic application beyond use as a metaphor for the correlation of symbolic activity and the effective integration of life force. In general, our consideration of the mind/body relationship is in terms of the body rather than in terms of a field of energy that is transcendent and encompasses the body. To take this step, we must open our senses to the perception of energy as the primary reality from which we approach therapy.

The concept of energy and higher sense perception (HSP) found in the discussion of chakras and auras from yogic and Taoist models have much to contribute to our therapeutic understanding and practice.

I recommend that we take the necessary steps to realize that spiritual energy is immediate, present, accessible, and usable. NFT uses symbolic and actual contact with the energy field to effectuate the therapeutic process. These energies are, in fact and practice, actual and discernable through the expanded development of our five senses. By extending and opening our perceptive range and sensitivities, we can:

- determine and deconstruct the beliefs and attitudes that countermand the sensibility of our faculties,

- do practices and activities that attune to and energize the relevant faculties,

- assume the reality of the faculty and practice refining our discernment, and

- test each new level of belief, skill, and understanding through a reductive protocol.

## NOETIC FIELD BALANCING

I developed noetic field balancing from the practice of balancing the human aura that I learned at Quimby Center. I use the word noetic because the dimensions of consciousness that we are able to access and affect therapeutically extend beyond the traditional concept of the aura. In practice, we link with the field of love and intelligence that forms the background movement of the therapeutic relationship. As Apostle Paul said, "Let the mind be in us that is in Jesus." We are using our spiritual mind to focus and cooperate with the spiritual intelligence that is implicit throughout the material, psychological, and spiritual realms. In the practice of noetic field balancing, therapy proceeds by focusing on energy first and image second. We reference our therapeutic attunement first on the energy field, followed by attention to the body and psychological structures.

In conventional practice, we have begun with the issue, explored its structure, and inferred the blockage in the intentional flow of energy. With NFT, we begin with the blockage of energy in the field itself as it exists around the physical body. Once the block is discerned and attuned to, we explore the related belief structure or complex. Blocks generally are beliefs that impede or distort actualization. They are choices that diminish our sense of self or separate us from our inherent goodness. Blocks stay in force because we believe in them. We assist clients to change, re-frame, or forgive themselves for the blocking beliefs or judgments. Concurrently, our therapeutic focus forms a conduit for the flow of spiritual energy (such as chi, dharma, or the Holy Spirit). This flow of energy helps release the blocks, and balances the noetic field. When the distortions are gone, the field is once again fluid and smooth. The field is energized, and the noetic field resumes its natural function of nourishing the body, protecting the psyche, integrating the body, mind, and soul, and maintaining a resonance with the noetic field.

## Analysis

The similarity of perturbations and the energy therapy reference to blocks and distortions is striking. TFT and Barbara Brennan's balancing the human energy field, and balancing the auric energy fields (as described in the *Auric Mirror*, by Ellavivian Power)—all are energy-field therapies. TFT and aura balancing specifically ask the client to attune to the perturbation, or block, as a means of accessing the field that needs transformation. Further, the cause of "cure" is the same. In both cases, the client attunes to blocking belief. In balancing, the client exercises self-forgiveness and/or awareness of the limiting choice, enabling higher consciousness to selectively act. The realignment in TFT appears to accomplish a similar freeing up and centering. In TFT, deconstruction occurs by loosening the block in the thought field by stimulating the associated meridians. In both cases, greater balance ensues as a result of the treatment. Whereas TFT seeks a relief of the symptom, NFT goes beyond relief to facilitate a greater sense of soul or self. Soul-space is a central concept in NFT and must be experientially real to the client and specifically accessed in relationship to the given issue, block, distortion, or perturbation. In phenomenological terms, the soul-space is the noesis of the noematic correlation with the noema, as issue, block, distortion, or perturbation.

Focus therapy, TFT and noetic field balancing follow the procedure of phenomenological reduction. The block, perturbation, or felt sense is the noema of the noematic correlation. The therapist assists the client to bracket—focus on the perturbation with the exclusion of all else. A sequence is followed that deconstructs the sedimenting field of beliefs, perceptions, and psychological forces. The center of awareness shifts to the noesis in the noematic correlation. In the inspirational state that Husserl called the "transcendental ego," the noesis is understood. From a therapeutic perspective, transformation occurs with the shift to

92

noesis. In focus therapy, this is the felt shift. In TFT, it is the relief of the perturbation, or "cure." I refer to this as the epiphany. In NFT, cure comes from changing one's relationship to the problem in a way that is freeing, rather than just processing the problem, which tends to reorganize the elements of distress with no resulting transformation. Analyzing or evaluating the problem expands the complex, whereas deconstruction frees us and enables us to access the truth that relates to the problem.

In this methodology, the consciousness and discipline of the practitioner is essential to the quality of the transformational experience. In reduction, the practitioner suspends beliefs, agendas, and expectations. The practitioner guides the client through a similar process. Transformation, or "cure," occurs when the client breaks free of the sedimenting beliefs surrounding the trauma. This approach works because all noematic forms, constructions, or circumstances refer to an intention that is imbedded in a deeper intentionality. A symptom simply described the experience of a deep intentional aim that is reversed, or blocked by a concept, belief or judgment. From the perspective of NFT, there is a greater field of consciousness that contains and assists the actualization of the individual. Perturbations, distortions, or blocks are adversarial constructions that separate our awareness and limit our access to the life giving noetic energy field. In NFT, cure occurs when the individual centers in the soul-space and accesses the noetic field relative to the presenting issue or sedimented belief structures related to the trauma. When we look at focus therapy, TFT, and noetic field balancing in the larger context, they are all forms of NFT.

I like to describe the experience of cure as an epiphany. In brief, epiphany is the coming of the Light. It is the experience of awakening as soul while still embedded in the therapeutic process. In TFT, a SUDs of 1 is considered a cure, no negative emotional response. The therapeutic sequence continues from the felt shift (focus therapy) into a confluence, or convergence, between the trauma and belief that was time-bound as a block, loosening the sedimentation, allowing the influx of eternity. The affect is usually described in soul terms such as joy, peace, love, enthusiasm, and compassion.

## Access

Accessing the noetic field can be simple.

1.  Focus on the image or statement that you want an answer for or want to understand.

2.  Inhale steadily and deeply while holding the noematic focus.

3.  When the in-breath is maximum, hold it and focus intently on the noema as long as you can.

4.  Rapidly release the breath and relax as totally as possible, simultaneously letting go of the breath and focus (deconstruction) releasing yourself into the noetic field.

5.  Settled in, describe your awareness of your present state or experience (noesis).

6.  Articulate what occurs to you (correlative state).

## ESSENTIAL UNDERSTANDING

The reality of self as a conscious energy field is essential to the understanding and the effective application of NFT, and how it fits into the range of psychological and spiritual cosmologies. This energy, though nonphysical, has a form of substance particular to the realm one is accessing. We have instruments that can detect some aspects of these subtle realities; however, our individual physical and spiritual functions, at present, make the best instruments. Equally helpful is our capacity to metaphorically extrapolate the models of physics. Though it is clear that the energy of physics is different from that of metaphysics, there is value in the symbolic connection of the two. However, from the perspective of quantum physics, the difference in the two energies is less clear. Whatever the case the concept of "energy" helps us articulate the noetic experiences. Just as the atom is theoretically inferred based on its effects, we can infer the soul based on its mental, emotional, and physical effects. Though our technology has not yet given us vision into the atom, with spiritual sight we can see into the world of the soul. Through eyes made of soul, we can look into the universe of the atom and know where to direct our technology and how to interpret the information we gather. As we unlock our soul vision, we find that we are also able to sense and interpret changes in this energy field through the interface of the dense and subtle forms of our nervous system and to perceive nonphysical realms. I suspect that at some point, we will discover that the energy of physics and metaphysics is the same.

## NFT Model

All noetic protocols begin with a prayer (silent or spoken) and an alignment with higher consciousness. As an enhanced form of rapport, the client enters the noetic field with the practitioner. This constitutes a shift into an altered state of consciousness that enhances the client's ability to access appropriate information, clarity, and forgiveness. The client may not be aware of this shift, so the practitioner must be adept at holding a witness, alignment, and focus. As the noetic field becomes more energized, the interface and the nexus points expand to include all senses, one or more inner senses, and HSP. In some ways, our entire consciousness and somatic sensitivity become avenues of perception.

## NEXUS POINTS

There are many nexus points. We will explore two in this discussion. One is the nexus to the noetic field. The other is within the therapeutic relationship. The nexus point that connects to higher consciousness is in the top of the head, while the nexus that engages the energy field of the client is in the forehead and often tracks with the physical vision and HSP (Higher Sense Perception). The forehead nexus is attention, and the top of the head nexus is intention. You maintain a simultaneous attentiveness with these nexus points while interacting with the therapeutic process as it presents itself. When using the forehead point in this way, be careful not to project into the field of the client. That action will tend to enmesh you in the client's energy, making it harder to maintain clear alignment and may confuse your energy and cause "compassion fatigue," or promote "counter-transference."

The development of the nexus points is important to your ability to use this therapy effectively. If this is an unfamiliar or uncomfortable viewpoint, you need not assume your nexus points are not active, that you lack aptitudes, or skill. A variety of religious, spiritual, counseling, and ethical practices promote the development of these points. Developing the observer, unconditional positive regard, rapport, intuition, phenomenological reduction, and transforming one's countertransference support the development of these centers. Years of impeccable experience based on spiritual values will enhance your development. NFT calls for you to initiate conscious, concerted attention to awakening, aligning, and centering in your soul-space, practicing NFT protocols, and doing regular spiritual practices.

## Dynamics

The following diagram charts the noetic relationship between the client and therapist. It can also be taken as a diagram of the relationship between any two people interested in assisting each other to transform a problematical situation or limiting belief. This is a dynamic relationship that brackets all, including the client and therapist. The witness and alignment of the practitioner is essential, because, the therapist must also deconstruct his/her own process and all beliefs and constructs concerning what we know or who we are and what we are doing, while remaining engaged with higher consciousness and the client.

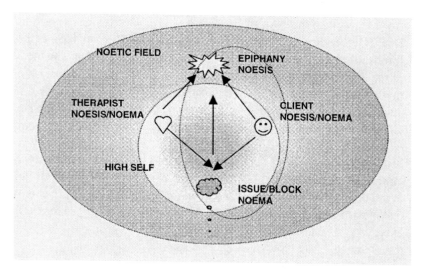

While the client deconstructs the sedimented belief (block/noema), you deconstruct any countertransference (noema). The epiphany occurs when the client accesses the noetic field through the focus of the client's issue (block). The practitioner's alignment and impeccability enhance the transformative experience.

The noetic field is accessed by the relationship of the practitioner, client, and higher consciousness. The presence of the noetic field is the basis for the learning or the therapeutic experience. The field is initiated by the connection of your focus, and increases in subtlety and power as the therapeutic process proceeds. Once the access to the noetic field is experientially created between you and the client, a realization emerges that the noetic field already existed as an infinite resource. Since this is an experiential discovery, you may have to accept the assertion that it works on faith. It will work, and, at some point, the experiential validation will emerge.

# PROTOCOLS

As we have discussed, we bind our energy through sequential processes. For that reason, the protocol of therapy may be more important than the content. The content certainly carries the frequency, or identification through which we locate and engage blocks. However, it is through our psychological traveling and re-sequencing through awareness and choice that we unfold the possibility of transformation. The following protocols have proven effective and useful in my practice.

## Alignment

The protocol for aligning to the noetic field and activating your attunement is simple. It requires that you focus your attention, visualizing each element as it is added, to the best of your ability, and relaxing and releasing everything else. The noetic field matches you according to your understanding, imagery, and intention. When you have difficulty sensing, seeing, or experiencing your relationship to the nexus and noetic field, then your faith, intention, and surrender will work. Remember, in your nexus with the noetic field, you are more intelligent and compassionate than you are as an ego self alone.

If the following protocol seems to be too much, instead: 1) be silent with your client for a moment, 2) honor his or her humanity, and 3) align yourself with unconditional positive regard.

The numbers in this protocol correspond to the same numbers in the illustration.

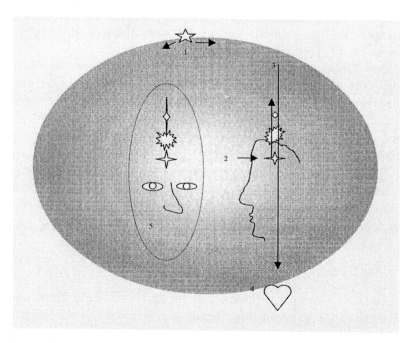

1.      In an attitude of reverence and surrender, begin with a prayer.
        Ask the higher power to be present and to surround you and the
        client, and surrender to that higher power. [The sequence is
        universal. Into this simple protocol, you insert the holy words
        that activate your attunement. A silent prayer is fine.]

2.      Place your attention at the center of your brow, through your
        brow into the center of your head, and imagine a point of light.
        [You may see or experience a quality of energy, color, symbol
        or sound.]

3.      Direct your attention from the center of your head through the
        top of your head. [At some point, the noetic field will engage
        this focus, signified by a symbol, felt sense, or experience that
        is consistent with your spiritual orientation or archetypal nature.
        I often see the Sanskrit word "Hu" or a dove with outstretched
        wings and head pointing toward the top of my head. To me,
        both signify the Holy Spirit.]

4.      Bring your attention down through the top and center of your
        head into your heart. [Regard your heart as a chalice filling with
        energy from the noetic field and    overflowing into your

relationship with the client. You may see something other than a chalice, but generally it will be a receptacle or receiving in nature.]

5.   Direct your attention to your client while maintaining an awareness of your alignment. [Your aligned attention to the client through the noetic field activates a *soul circle*, which is a circular energy that links the soul of the client and the practitioner and contains the therapeutic process. It is a deep level of rapport.]

## Reductive Focus

The *reductive focus protocol* unlocks sedimented beliefs or blocks. The sequence creates the necessary conditions for transformation and facilitates alignment with the soul.

As you practice the protocol and develop the skill of reduction, your mind develops into a perceptual organ of the soul. (Husserl did not use this exact description for his experience. He did, however, know he was changed by the practice of his philosophy of science.)

1.   Begin with the alignment protocol.

2.   Focus on the selected phenomenon (noema), excluding all else.

3.   Deconstruct the sedimentation of beliefs, loosening your perceptual fixity.

4.   Experientially discern the meaning (noesis).

## Universal

The *universal protocol* provides a framework for applying techniques and procedures from compatible models that incorporate some form of reduction.

1.   Begin with the alignment protocol.

2.   Focus on cure as a soul-centering intentionality that is indexed to the issue or symptom.

3.      Apply the technique, procedure, or protocol.

## Foundation

The *foundation protocol* assists the client to move from a self-image, belief, or ego-center defined by external circumstances to a soul-centered knowing based on the experience of one's inherent goodness. The issue does not disappear. It remains worthy of consideration but no longer defines or dominates one's center.

1.      Begin with the universal protocol.

2.      Ask what the client is experiencing (felt sense).

3.      Ask the client to take a breath, clear the air (energy field), and sharpen the focus on the reported experience.

4.      Make a focusing statement. [For example, "Tell me a time when you tried to share your loving and couldn't." You may also perceive an image or have a sense, hunch, or insight from which you can form a focus statement. The client's insights may also serve to make focusing comments. The client may report information concerning an issue or a concern.]

5.      Bring attention to or touch the point in the energy field around the client that expresses the distortion or block, or have the client touch the physical location. If nothing is apparent, just be present.

6.      Assist the client to access and describe the traumatic moment: who did what to whom? Or, on the basis of that experience, how did the client diminish, judge, demean, or shame him-/herself (noema)? Assist the client in self-forgiveness or reframe the judgment. [Audibly stating the forgiveness is important. A statement affirming one's self and the particular denied or suppressed virtue in relationship to the event is often a powerful support to the forgiveness process (reduction).]

7.      Ask the client to take a deep breath to facilitate the release and the receptiveness to a response from higher consciousness.

8.    Ask the client to give permission for higher consciousness or the Holy Spirit to touch into that injury or place of need and to give permission for that place to respond to that spiritual help.

10.   Hold the space, and encourage the client to let go and follow the flow of the epiphany (noesis).

## Insightful Focus

Not withstanding that the road to mastery can be long and challenging, accessing the noetic field can be simple. In fact, it needs to be simple so that you can readily explore NFT. The *insightful focus protocol* is a simple way to access information from the noetic field. It was developed from transcendental phenomenology, follows the same steps as the reductive focus protocol, and is used to align or bring insight to you and the client.

1.    Focus on the image or statement that you want an answer for or understanding of (noema).

2.    Inhale steadily and deeply while holding the noetic focus.

3.    When the in-breath is maximum, hold it and focus intently on the noema.

4.    Rapidly release the breath, and relax as totally as possible letting go of the focus and releasing yourself into the noetic field (reduction).

5.    Relax further while you allow understanding or insight to emerge (noesis).

6.    Articulate (speak or journal) whatever occurs to you.

## Re-Placing

In his book, *Look to the Mountain*, Greg Cajete, a foremost Native American scholar from the Santa Clara Pueblo in New Mexico, discusses the importance of place in indigenous learning. We speak of making a place for ourselves or finding our place. In the Native

American experience, place is fundamental to a healthy spiritual and psychological orientation.

In the therapeutic relationship, I observed that clients were required to give up who they were to get shelter, safety, nurture, esteem, or survival. They literally and symbolically had to give part of themselves to someone else who controlled what they needed. They had to relinquish their sense of place to be acculturated. Instead of the client having a sense of themselves in their own center or soul-space, the controlling person was in that space dictating how, and what they should be. They had to "sell out" to bond themselves, so to speak. It was apparent to me that my clients had given away their space to the point of having lost their sense of owning their life or being their own person. They had no grounding. Symptomatically, they expressed this as feeling of not belonging here, as if they were dropped from a space ship, illegitimate, or orphaned.

When one's sense of place is not sufficient, higher levels of integration appear to be limited. There is no place, in one's center or space, to anchor higher consciousness. Therapeutic changes do not seem to hold or work at all when the client's sense of place is insufficient. Without the compass provided by place, actualization is difficult and transformation is curtailed. The *re-placing protocol* strengthens the client's sense of place by retrieving, realigning, and reintegrating the "given-away self" with a place or center in present time. This technique is extremely helpful in situations of sexual abuse. Often the sense of one's self as victim, or one's self a permanently damaged, can not be resolved until after the effective use of the *re-placing* technique.

1.   Find the initiating events when you gave a part of yourself away in exchange for safety, survival, power, nurture, esteem, or shelter.

2.   Forgive yourself for abandoning or betraying yourself, and affirm yourself as your center.

3.   Locate the symbolic self, that you actually gave away, in the field or image of the predatory person, that you "gave" the specific aspect of yourself away to. [Your self-image will appear embedded in the energy field or body of the other person.]

4.   Begin a slow breath, and visualize the self you gave away that is embedded in the field of the predator. [It may appear as an image of you, color, shadow, or symbol. Your best criteria is that it seems like you and not the predator.]

5.   As you continue the slow in-breath, see the given-away self traveling from the control person to you and entering through the top of your head into your physical body. It will go to its rightful place.

6.   As you complete the breath, visualize the given-away self and the physical self-of-now in the same simultaneous place.

7.   Hold your breath and continue visualizing both physical forms as one.

8.   Rapidly exhale, let go, and totally relax. [The retrieved element merges with you in the present.]

9.   Assess the field of the predator for other remnants of your self. When all are retrieved the predator will appear to recede, diminish or dissolve in some way. This indicates they no longer have a hold on you.

## Making Even

I became aware of another perplexing issue similar to place. My usual approach either did not work or had minor effect. There was no evident shift in the client's felt sense or experience of self. I suspected that the blocks I had been addressing were an effect of a deeper concern or that a priority agenda held those forms in place.

I discovered that many times the priority agenda was some form of revenge. As long as the client wanted revenge, nothing would release, transform, or cure. Higher consciousness was unable or not permitted to assist. The target of the revenge can be someone else or one's self. It may look like "living up to someone else's expectations," or "proving oneself." Revenge holds a client in dualistic consciousness and, as such, prevents noetic-field access and soul-space alignment. Higher consciousness, being noninflictive and nonadversarial, has to stand by and cannot act as long as the client wants revenge.

We have a natural instinct to make ourselves whole. As a reversal of the natural instinct, revenge is an adversarial approach, which perpetuates wounding. When we center in our wound, wholeness becomes out of our reach. In contrast to "getting even," the *making even protocol* helps make whole.

1.   Trace the early trauma.

2.   Experience and own your victimization.

3.   Accept the anger and rage resulting from the violation.

4.   Determine whether the vengeful acts were directed at self or another.

5.   Decide if you want to surrender your desire for revenge. If you give up your desire for revenge, you are not condoning the perpetrating behavior but changing your relationship to it. [As long as you want revenge the perpetrator controls your state of being. By wanting revenge, you perpetrate their action on yourself over and over. They only did it to you once.]

6.   Forgive yourself for making revenge more important than the liberation of your own soul.

7.   Allow the energy flow to complete itself while giving permission to your hurt place to receive spiritual intervention and give permission to the higher consciousness (Holy Spirit, Great Spirit, noetic field, universal compassion) to assist you deeply in your transformation. Have compassion for the victimizer.

8.   Articulate any change in your subjective experience.

9.   Check and see if there are remaining or additional elements of yourself embedded in the perpetrator's field. If so, repeat the process. If yes, use the Re-Placing protocol.

If appropriate, return to the original technique or procedures that appeared ineffective and that initially suggested revenge was the priority agenda and try it again. You can also combine this process with the *re-placing* protocol.

## Time Angel

The past continually cycles into the present. As we engage present challenges, we are also healing our past. We can translate current events into metaphor and look for causation in the past. When the past trauma awakens in our emotions and in our somatic memory, awareness brings transformation. As we deepen our awareness of self as energy, we become aware of a greater power for change within our noetic field.

Our vision of our past is very much alive within us. We can move noetically to any time or place when we once needed help. We still need the help. The goal is not to change the event. It is to change the quality of the event and our relationship to it. In a sense, as we interpret events and form our beliefs about ourselves in those events, we create holographic beings who are replicas of ourselves at those times. This phenomenon is similar to Callahan's "holons." When these *orphans* were created with insufficient loving, a vital aspect of our life force is caught in the dimension of the past. Once created, the location of these "holographic orphans" is in the unconscious field around your physical body.

In this protocol, the client is guided through a journey to her past. The goal of the journey is to find her orphans who needed someone like herself to be present, supportive, engaged, and loving. You can also use this protocol on yourself. To make it easier to read, the *time angel protocol* is presented as if to a female client. If appropriate, re-cast as a male client.

1.  Relax and close your eyes while we ask for the presence of the Holy Spirit or the Light for the highest good. [Essentially, this is a prayer for guidance, protection, healing, and engaging the noetic field at a level that knows the highest good of the client and the practitioner.]

2.  Imagine that you are traveling into your past. In this journey, you are looking for past selves who needed you as you are now. The goal is to be your self-of-now with your self-of-then. At some point, you will sense or see the self-of-then that needs you. Take your time. Observe.

3.    As your self-of-then becomes clearer, describe that persona as distinct from the self-of-now, i.e., what is she wearing, what is on her feet, etc? How is her hair fixed? How old . . . , what fragrances . . . , time of day . . . , inside . . . , outside . . . , time of year . . . ? Engage all your senses.

4.    When your self-of-then becomes clear and more delineated and seems to take on a substance, a reality, see your self-of-now and your self-of-then together in that place and time. Be cautious. Give your self-of-then time to respond. She may be timid or somewhat frightened. If she does not recognize you, introduce yourself. Explain that you are her self-of-the-future and that you are there to help.

5.    Slowly wait for her to approach you or begin to relax with your presence. See if you can reach out and touch her. If touch is allowed, explore holding her in your arms and fill her with your loving. This may take awhile.

6.    When you sense that the loving is working, invite your self-of-then, if it seems appropriate, to forgive herself for any way that she believes she is unlovable, powerless, or inadequate because of the current circumstances or anything that may have happened. Have her forgive herself for any self-shame or blame. After the forgiveness, have her let it all go and fill those spaces with more loving.

7.    When the time seems right, tell your self-of-then that you must return to your time. Tell her that she can call you whenever she needs you. Or, she can return to the present with you, knowing that the two of you will merge.

8.    Return to the present, take a deep breath, and see yourself as a light body containing your physical body. Be aware of what you are experiencing, and slowly open your eyes.

The name of this protocol honors an experience that I had with a client. When she was a small child, she was locked away in a room. The room was warm enough. She had a bed. Food was left for her, and she had a pot that she could use as a toilet. As I was guiding her in this process, we were just at the point when I said, "Now have the self-of-now enter the room with the self-of-then." She suddenly exclaimed, "Oh! I'm the one!" She said she survived those times because an angel had come to her. The angel held her and filled her with loving. When I had her enter the room, she said that she realized that the angel who had come to her was herself.

All the faculties are present in adult life to travel the time line as it is imaged into the holographic meaning-structures within the individual. Awakening to the transcendental dimension is like being "born again" into our wholeness. Time travel allows us to heal and transform our past, which creates a present that is as if we had lived the healed past. In a manner of speaking, we become our own parents. We move as the soul-of-itself and enter into whatever the time-bound self needs. As we awaken into the depth and wholeness of who we are, the events and beliefs appear in perspective. We see our life as a continual enhancement of the soul.

### Structural Symbolic Focusing

Each consciousness center, or chakra, differentiates in its psychospiritual function into specialized areas. Each center serves the soul's activity in specialized ways. As a result, each center will characteristically contain blocking beliefs related to those functions. For example, when we try to share our loving and cannot, the beliefs we form in response to that trauma become blocks in the energy field near the heart center.

Begin with the alignment protocol. Each of the following focus statements provides a point of engagement. The focus statement draws a response from the client. This is an associative or resonant response, so whatever occurs to the client provides the next step. The focus statement and resonant response engages the intelligence and compassion of the noetic field. The focus statements are arranged in a particular sequence to optimize the therapeutic development of the energy field. For that reason, I recommend that you guide your progression according to the sequence given.

Insert each of the following focus statements into step four of the Foundation protocol. As content emerges, make any minor modifications that enable the process. Complete the entire foundation protocol for each block that emerges.

**Solar plexus.** Tell me about a time when you were alone, afraid, abandoned, hurt or experienced guilt or shame.

**Feet and knees.** Tell me about a time when you were confused or didn't understand, felt unsupported, had no sense of place or didn't belong.

**Spleen and root.** Tell me about a time when you judged your sexuality or creativity, had resentment, or needed revenge.

**Heart.** Tell me about a time when you had regret, felt disappointed or betrayed, or tried to share your loving and couldn't.

**Throat and mouth.** Tell me about a time when you had difficulty speaking or because you spoke.

**Eyes and ears.** Tell me about a time when you saw or heard something that was painful, disturbing, or frightening.

When you are sensitive to the energy field, you will be aware of, or sense, the realignment of the client into soul-space and the enhanced flow of energy. Asking clients what they are experiencing provides a reference point and anchors the transformation. Depending on the level of therapy, this protocol may not require specific attention to each center. Rapport in the noetic field while asking the focus statements may be sufficient.

## Symbolic Resonance

*Symbolic resonance* is a term I borrowed from Roger Wolger and his approach to regression therapy (past life). Simply stated, symbols resonate like piano strings: a note struck in one octave will resonate with the same note in another octave. The resonant consciousness opens memory fields from the past. The past experience appears as a structure in the field forming as an intentionality that we must fulfill or complete in a present experience. The symptom is a resonant call to the past for awareness, fulfillment, and transformation.

For example, I was listening to a client's story. We had approached her situation from several perspectives, and nothing seemed to help. I suspected something deeper. As I listened, I heard the phrase "No matter what I do, it will never be enough." I asked her to close her eyes and repeat the phrase, letting go of anything else that tried to catch her attention. She said she experienced an inner vision, which appeared to be a past-life metaphor. She saw herself as a small child. Her mother had died and her father did what he could but did not have much time for her. She felt alone, abandoned, and unwanted—insufficient for meeting life's challenges. I asked her to go to her time of death. She found herself hovering over her corpse which had a sword piercing her neck into her shoulder. She had also complained of neck and shoulder pain. Her dying thought was, "Whatever I do, I will never be enough."

She had an element of revenge as well. In this case, she directed it toward herself. I always treat "past lives" as accurate and an appropriate metaphor. By doing so, I can avoid deciding whether or not it was an actual past life or whether not we had past lives, and get on with the therapeutic process. As my teacher used to say, "We have to spend our eternity somewhere."

In summary, the protocol is:

1. Listen for the resonant phrase.

2. Direct the client to focus on it, and with closed eyes, repeat it over and over until it elicits a felt shift or image. Have the client articulate the felt sense and image.

3. Elaborate until epiphany occurs.

4. Elaborate in terms of understanding and current circumstances.

5. Conduct self-forgiveness, if appropriate.

## Enfolding and Unfolding Holiness

Our place, and the space it circumscribes, is our *sphere of influence.* We enfold time, as we live it, into an implicate order of our place. The past is an implicate dimension of the present. In the geometrical context of self awareness as place, we are implicated in a greater presence of a transpersonal self, a soul-self. Our soul implicates and transcends our time bound self as spatial context. This is the essence of transformation.

Through the vehicle of self, we can unfold specific implicate realms within. We can all enfold our awareness into these inner dimensions. Self as nexus is our gateway to our inner worlds. We began to develop these aspects of self while exploring the inner dimensions of self, as holy space, as inner teacher. Once linear, our foot prints appear in all times and places at once.

# REFERENCES

Assagioli, R. *Psychosynthesis. New York: Viking Press, 1974.*

Callahan, R J. And J Callahan. *Thought Field Therapy and Trauma: Treatment and Theory.* Indian Wells, Ca: Thought Field Therapy Training Center, 1996

Hinterkopf, E. *Integrating Spirituality in Counseling: A Manual for Using Experiential Focusing Method.* Alexandria, VA: American Counseling Association, 1998.

Ihde, D. *Experimental Phenomenology.* New York: Putnam, 1977. York: Bollingen Foundation, 1960.

Jung, C G. *On the Nature of the Psyche.* New York.

Maslow, A H. *The Farther Reaches of Human Nature.* New York: Viking Press, 1971.

Waterman, R. D. *Eyes Made of Soul: Theory and Practice of Noetic Field Therapy.* Santa Fe: RDW, 1999.

# Chapter Six

# NOETIC FIELD THERAPY

The application of the curative nature of the noetic field is ancient, finding modern expression in spiritual healing, prayer therapy, therapeutic touch, chi-gung, acupuncture, and shamanism. Classically called the human aura, this energy field is biblically referred to as a *halo, radiance,* or *countenance.* Yoga psychology views the energy field as an aura surrounding the body, interacting through spiritual and psychological levels via structures called chakras. An increasing interest in spiritual counseling, complementary medicine, quantum physics, and cross-cultural shamanism has broadened our professional capacity to consider the legitimacy of self as energy and the therapeutic implications of that understanding. In a real sense, as we expand our understanding and our own organism as a refined sensory array, we come to view healing, psychological transformation, and transcendental discovery as a *spiritual physics.*

Though there is a growing interest in energy psychology and medicine, sceptics continue to be cautious, even adversarial. While a growing contingent of physicists lobby for a physics that includes consciousness, spiritual scientists continue to develop rigorous protocols through which consciousness can be explored through human awareness. However, there is some basis for caution. We must always account for the shadow side of any practice, wisdom, or set of beliefs. Energy therapy is not excluded. In fact, the more dogmatic, the more the caution. The greater the power and ego-inflation, the greater potential for ethical deception. Some try to discredit energy therapy as being "new age," "too much on the fringe," "un-scientific," or "the devils work." These are all the same criticism. It is all about power, control, and dominance as an acceptable means to feel safe in our own beliefs, even though these practices hurt others and further separate us from our truth, and the truth of our natural holiness.

Just as there is resistance by some public and professional viewpoints, there are as many, or more, who are ready for a broader, more comprehensive approach to life. We are in the midst of a cultural phenomenon called a "paradigm shift" in which collective humanity calls for a social transformation to an ecological and sustainable lifestyle. Energy therapy in general, and Noetic Field Therapy in particular, is on the cutting edge of this change.

## NATURE OF NOETIC FIELD

The traditional name for our energy field is the human aura. Based on my experience as a therapist and discovery as a researcher, this terms seems limited. The *aura* is an energy field that appears to exist within a larger array of forces, that affect its healthy function. The *noetic field* is a broader concept, that brings to our awareness the deeper dimension of spiritual essence and mastery implied by the understanding of self as energy and holiness. Our "space" is our self as energy, holding and containing our embodied. Noetic takes our awareness to the dimension of soul. Soul has dominion over our thoughts, images, feelings, and physical states. This dominion functions through a life-span archetypal structure of intentionality, or destiny. For the most part this level of awareness remains unconscious, only showing itself through inspirational moments, and life transitions. As we more consciously choose the inner directiveness of essence, the power of our soul extends into a direct influence on our daily thoughts and actions. We gradually prefer life from a soul-centered perspective, and subsume our ego into middle management. We integrate our personality with soul. The noetic field unfolds from the soul and also enfolds the soul. Our noetic nature is our nexus with soul and our soul contains our noetic nature. When we apply our consciousness to the balance and alignment of this energy field, we are changing the field by changing the context in which it exists in relationship to the core nature, and alignment, of the individual we are working with. Because of the scope of this endeavor, our alignment and spiritual access, as practitioner, is crucial to the effectiveness of the therapy.

The aura, or energy field, surrounds and penetrates the physical body. As a more encompassing concept, the noetic field surrounds and interpenetrates this auric energy field. Historically, artists depict halos around the heads of individuals to denote their spirituality. Biblically, writers refer to the "raiment" or "countenance of light" in an attempt to describe the field of spiritual energy around angels, men, and women. We use common-sense terms such as "blue mood," "red with anger," "green with envy," "full of energy," "radiant beauty," and "vibrant personality." Such terms are similar to how individuals with spiritual sight describe the energy field. It is common sense that we all have an unconscious awareness of our multidimensional connection to life.

Quantum physics describes the universe as energy. Energy and matter are interchangeable. Psychology, Eastern therapy, and complementary medicine have terms for life as energy. Some of the more well-known are "prana" (yoga), "chi" (acupuncture and chi-gung), "libido" (Western psychology), "orgon" (Reichian bioenergetics), "Holy Spirit" (Christianity), and "light" (universal spirituality).

## Mystery of the Cross

The noetic field, including what the ancients call the aura, is a dynamic system of contexts and relationships. The refinement of our psychological construction is a key to the balance and alignment of these systems. The next consideration is that of energy. We have explored this to some extent. The cross is an ancient symbol for the interaction between the vertical access to the spiritual dimension and the horizontal actualization of life in this three dimensional world. This world is our experience of resolving the cause and effect of our soul's journey. It is through the interaction of the "cross" that we balance our psyche through application of noetic field balancing. This is what I am calling the *mystery of the cross*. So in a biblical sense, we resurrect the Christ within us through our sacrifice on the cross of life.

There is an ongoing discussion as to whether the use of the term energy is appropriate for talking about spiritual phenomenon and implicate realities. I have played with this at great length. Often I highlight the metaphoric value of the term energy. Our minds are accustomed to the seemingly concrete terms for energy and energy fields, such as those caused by magnetism and electricity. The truth is, we understand electricity and magnetism in operational terms; that is, by our description of its effect, i.e., electricity lights the bulb, or spinning the conductor around a magnet produces a current. We can effectively proceed and predict outcomes within limited parameters of what we believe the reality to be. The heart of why, or how, they work is mysterious. For now, I will settle for operational constructs. This means, we can use the term energy, given that we are clear about the referential context and set of relationships. When I use the term energy, I strive to provide a sufficient reference point from which our intelligence can proceed. My use of energy enables me to predict results, to "light the bulb," or "to make current."

The cross is an appropriate symbol for energy in terms of the ancient mysteries and our noetic development. In the emerging course of this writing, noetic appears as the synthesis of ancient mystery and modern perceptions shaped by psychology and physics.

Basically the vertical element of the cross is the central access of energy that links "heaven" and "earth," or, in physics, the implicate and explicate order. It represents the energy that we source from spirit, or Holy Spirit, the pure energy that unfolds from the "nothingness." It is the energy that moved the first creation into form, the nous, the voice, or wind of spirit. It is also the return, the call to truth, essence, and return to source, or home. It is the holiness that operates through an agreement, respect, honoring, unconditional love, and reverence for all life. It is the vertical axis of our center, as the flow of light through us between heaven and earth.

The horizontal bar of the cross is the "magnetic energy," the energy of life from within creation. Spirit structured into a context creates the magnetic energy. Depending on the structure, it attracts similar forms, i.e., we are attracted to places we like, and magnets attract iron. We might say that when we free ourselves from limitation through transformation or inspiration, we feel on fire. In an analogous way fire is freeing the spirit in the substance we are burning. From burning coal to accessing the archetypes of personal power, patriotism or religious zealotry, what I am calling magnetic energy can be accessed regardless of the quality of our consciousness, or good or evil intent. We can use it freely based on choice, whether in adversity, domination or coercion, or protection, safety, or health. It also represents the actualizing vector of soul-fulfillment. The horizontal movement of the soul is the actualization of our life-span agendas.

The cross symbolizes that our center and balance in life is the equality of the horizontal and vertical experience. In the spiritual worlds, we are spirit. In this world, we are spirit and matter. Psychological stress, and imbalance in the energy field, reflect a distorted or imbalanced cross. When the aura is balanced, we become centered and radiant.

When I speak of the noetic field, the implication is that its energy is also a commingling of intelligence and love. The mystery of this love and intelligence begins in our initial awareness of polarities and contrast, and evolves into the inclusion of tertiary associations. As we explored earlier, any duality, dichotomy, polarity has a third element of unity. The evolution of our life and intelligence progresses through contrast and shifts into noetic understanding as we experience this third pole of reality. The duality is the magnetic and the trinity is the vertical, or spiritual. The magnetic provides the visibility of the spiritually invisible. The cross also symbolizes the purposefulness of our life expression. The cross symbolizes the intelligence of evolution through loving.

## Noetic Levels

The study of this material is interesting from a content level. More important, however, is the impact that it has on our perception as we reflect on the concepts, information, and the patterns that they make. By involving ourselves with this material, our perception increasingly shifts, gradually enabling us to look deeper into the human psyche and begin to understand consciousness as it presents itself in human form. The activity of reflecting, contemplating, and associating develops a new lens of perception. Though it is an invitation to study these models more deeply, at some point, however, our journey must carry us to an awareness beyond structure where energy is the texture of the mystery. The resonance of the material acts on deep structures, awakening genetic patterns, enabling us to look through eyes made of soul.

The following figure is a beginning representation of the noetic field's dynamic structure. The diagram shows the physical body and its relationship to the chakras, or energy centers. Each center correlates with specific psychological functions: *Root* is energy and support; *Sacral* is creativity and sexuality; *Solar Plexus* is power, security and belonging, and; *Heart* is love, courage and relationship; *Throat* is communication and symbolic awareness; *Brow* is seeing; *Crown* is perception and transpersonal awareness. I added a center at the feet to represent the chakra of *place*. I did this because of the dynamic of belonging and its powerful effect on the entire field. Also, I added a transcendent chakra. This chakra is our nexus with spirit, a holy place where we "worship spirit in spirit." For now, we can call this the *I Am* chakra. It also allows us to operate in the dynamics of self that are independent of the time-space continuum of our everyday life. Of course, there are more dimensions. These are the primary dimensions that directly relate to balancing.

The two interlaced triangles are the integration of above and below. They are the two-dimensional image for the star-tetrahedron, which, in turn, is the sacred geometry of our light-body. *Spiritual Physics* is the application of sacred geometry. Our multidimentional

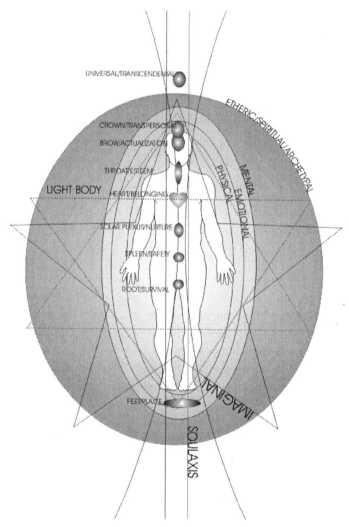

nature is expresses as geometry. When we organize our psychology according to outer indices, the light-body slows and dims, and our DNA re-sequences itself to density. When we organize our psychology according to our light-body, our DNA sequences to its inherent, natural rhythm of light. The curved lines reflect the universal flow of magnetic and spiritual *light* and *sound* as it "breathes" through the geometric, vertical, mental, emotional, imaginal, and physical expression. This can also be depicted as a column of light through the vertical axis of the body and personal space. Subjectively, we identify the phenomenon of the vertical axis phenomenon as "our center." The purpose of it all is to provide experience to our souls. In the last chapter, we will explore this center as a conduit of access to higher consciousness.

Each level of consciousness develops from a root pattern of archetypes. These root patterns act like a mirror for the denser energy. Our health is based on how truly our lives resonate with these archetypal genetics. Healing is a matter of bringing imbalances into a healthy resonance with the root pattern, or genetic archetype. The needed pattern could be provided by a substance, ritual, or a change in understanding. Spirit, being the essence of all root patterns, is able to balance any pattern, provided it does not violate the free choice and path of the individual creator, or the integrity of the primary pattern of the whole.

"Chakra," a Sanskrit word meaning "wheel," is a central organizing principle of yoga psychology. The function of each chakra matches the levels of meaning in Maslow's hierarchy of needs, from a Western psychological approach. Huna is an indigenous approach to the same realities, developed by the ancient Hawaiians and continued by native and nonnative Kahuna practitioners. The psychosynthesis model was developed by Assagioli from his study of esoteric wisdom and experience as a psychotherapist. By overlaying the map of depth psychology onto the human energy fields and using the physical body as our point of reference, we can visually and imaginally explore the psycho-spiritual structures as relationships of energy. The preceding diagram presents these levels. Maslow's hierarchy of needs and the chakras appear in the vertical axis of the body. The levels of psychological functioning extend in contours from the body. Locally, the energy field is limited to our own space. Internally, each center is structurally vast.

The psychological functions are interactive levels. These levels are *physical, etheric, imaginal, emotional, mental, archetypal,* and *spiritual.* We will explore these levels as structural dynamics that influence the flow of energy (or consciousness) in and around the physical body. Within these levels is a realm of consciousness that I call *soul-space.*

Soul-space is our refuge within ourselves, ground of being, and source to spirit. For most, awareness of this space begins as myth. It is ephemeral. Conceptually, we may believe that we are inherently spiritual. Our soul-space grows as we reflect on our essence as spiritual, develop an observer relationship to our issues, traumas, and habits, meditate and pray more often, and forgive ourselves more readily. As we transform our experience and awaken spiritually, our soul-space grows. At some point, we realize we are soul living as the presence of peace, joy, love, grace, wisdom, and power. Solving our problems begins to seem less important than developing a soul relationship to our problems. We no longer define ourselves in terms of external viewpoints. Shame or blame may persist to a degree but it no longer forms any aspect of who we are. Our identity is in the realm of soul while our life in the world continues to interface through the province of the ego. Whereas ego was once given ascendancy, it is now demoted to middle management.

The etheric body is sometimes referred to as the "etheric double" because it is a template or archetype for the physical body. It appears as an energy matrix. From one perspective, this system is described in chi-gung as the meridians of the body that transmit chi to the organs. The flow of chi is the flow of life force that maintains the health of the body. Eventually these meridians merge with the axial tonal lines that, as we develop, form a nexus with the universal flow of cosmic energy. The balance and alignment of the aura affects the functioning of the meridians. The chakras are a complementary structure to the meridians. Whereas the meridians interact with the organs of the body, the chakras interact with the endocrine system and nerve plexus. For all practical purposes, the etheric level of the aura is a subtle complement to the physical body.

**Physical.** Penetrates the physical and etheric bodies and reflects the state of the energy fields. When this level has a smooth, strong flow of energy, the body can accommodate enhanced forces deeper in the psyche. This level reflects physical trauma, cell memory, physical health, and somatogenic beliefs and emotions.

**Etheric Double.** A subtle counterpart of the physical body (not shown) that functions as an archetypal pattern or blueprint for the physical body. The meridians and chakras appear in this formation.

**Imaginal.** I depicted the imaginal level as a five pointed star because of the way it functions in the field. It is a function of creativity, thus it formulates relationship interdimensionally. It is the medium through which we create and transform our circumstances; sometimes called the "astral" level. This level can be developed as a function of perception or inner seeing, intention, and creativity. It is also highly susceptible to delusion. Excessive fantasy, created out of recreational drug use, or an intention to escape or avoid, can create forms in the aura that are

118

disconnected from the authentic processes of creativity. As a consequence, inner realities are created that are disconnected from the ability to complete, fulfill, or enhance the soul's purposes. In other words, these forms effectively help us avoid life and the challenges and rewards that our soul is destined to fulfill.

The imaginal level develops into a highly integrative and creative ability, serving shamanistic, transcendental, and actualizing purposes. Much of art therapy works through the power of this level.

This level is balanced as part of the physical and emotional balancing. Drug residues tend to be part of the physical level, and fantasy, in the emotional level. Keep in mind that the levels of the aura penetrate and ride across each other. For therapeutic purposes, we learn to focus our attention on one level at a time. This provides a type of separation due to our focus on one level. To work with each respective level, we focus on that level. By doing so, our consciousness excludes everything else that is not our focus.

Delusions and obsessions are generated through and reflected in this level. On the other hand, intention, positive self-image, image dialogue, construction and integration through imagery (as in psychosynthesis), visual learning, visualization and healing, manifestation, and success are all generated and reflected by this level. Used dissociatively, the imaginal level can be devastating. Used integratively, it is a powerful force for connecting, integrating, and aligning all the levels.

**Emotional.** Carries the artifacts of our feelings and emotional reactions and actions. Our emotions give life to our beliefs and judgments and the impetus to pursue our vision. For this reason, this level reflects an aspect of our dharma or causal body. "Causal" is translated from Eastern systems as the karmic-dharmic expression of our soul. It is the force that determines and sets the causation into our lives.

From that perspective, when we are neutral, we might assume we are not creating karma (actions that end in results.) We may also not be creating at all.

A more effective way to keep this level healthy, vital, balanced, and karma-free is through powerful, universally oriented, non-manipulative, and unconditionally loving. The destiny aspect of our causal nature is reflected through the archetypal level.

This level is the source of our drive for power and dominance. It powers our adversarial and competitive nature. It also is the source of passion, the total embracing, and the loving heart that heals and forgives. It reflects our warmth, our devotion, and what we care about. It is also the peacemaker. Our emotional level registers our fulfillment and longs for peace.

**Mental.** Reflects our beliefs, concepts, and attitudes. Though feelings and emotions are often keys to beliefs, our mental activity decides what we will build as our internal structure and how we will project ourselves into life. Through our mentality, we construct our relationship to our destiny, karma, and inner life. Balancing the mental aura is most similar to conventional depth and ego psychotherapy. Through our instinct for preservation, we take our beliefs as truth, as permanent, as the pillars of our existence. As a spiritual activity, beliefs are a practice of simulated realities serving transitory purposes. Some beliefs are couched in duality and cause us to resist and battle with ourselves. All beliefs ultimately serve as stepping stones to our enlightenment. Forgiveness is a key force in mental balancing: receiving forgiveness, forgiving others, and, most importantly, forgiving ourselves.

The mind is the constructor, the builder. This level reflects our associative activity through which we internalize and develop our integrative learning and personality. It is also dissociative and reflects the constraints that divide us from and within ourselves, and from each other. We shape our reality with our minds. Mental health or illness is reflected in this level. The capacity of the mind ranges from instinctive-intellectual to intuitive-reflective thinking. At the highest level, the spiritual intellect of cosmic consciousness or enlightenment merges the personal intellect with the superconscious, divine mind.

A main premise of this writing is that our minds are ripe for an evolutionary morphogenesis. As we shift from ego- to spiritual-mind (noetic), we activate our genetic structure and reach into a deeper level of our human potential.

**Archetypal.** Contains the map of our destiny; sometimes called the "etheric level" because it is the template or matrix for existence as an extension of our soul. Brennan calls this level "ketheric." I have heard it described as a "cosmic mirror" on which our life plan is imprinted. The soul sits on the other side, looking at life as through a one-way mirror, living in paradise, radiating into life through the patterns of destiny. From the ego's perspective, we only see the reflected light of the soul and the shadows of our destiny. The scenario symbolically portrayed on this mirror reflects into our mental, emotional, and physical lives as our destiny. It is much like a spiritual genetic code. When our

120

lives reflect given states of consciousness, or the accomplishment of certain lessons, adjustment is then permitted in the archetypal field. The archetypal level changes when we put in our time, pass the test, or awaken to the soul.

When reflected outside of us, we see the archetypes as the pantheon of gods. When internalized, these archetypes are the angels of destiny, the gods that dwell within us. It is the structure of intentionality.

Each culture has its mythology. Archetypal forces tend to dominate the personality until one's experience and development secures one in a sense of soul. When this happens, inner wars subside and cooperation between the internal and transcendental archetypes occurs. As this transformation occurs inwardly, peace is possible in social, economic, and political manifestation.

Archetypes form the themes of our lives individually and collectively. Events symbolically reflect inner processes. The symbolic and archetypal formation reflects themes that portray destiny. As life-long learning, our destiny is synonymous with our soul's curriculum. We came into life with an internal, archetypal lesson plan. At the archetypal level, we choreograph the mind, emotions, and imagination and physical actions. We transform the archetypes that contain and drive our expression. When we become conscious of ourselves as a soul-self, we transcend and master these powerful forces. As our awareness of the soul-self increases, we become a conscious executive capable of coordinating and experiencing reality beyond these archetypes, while living through them.

The archetypal level is our unconscious. There is collaboration in human activity through the collective unconsciousness. As individuals awaken to their inner realms, beyond the collective and archetypal ceilings, the collective is transformed. The phrase, "If I can be lifted up, I will draw others to me," is more than a dusty Biblical admonition. It is a strategy for social transformation. The archetypal level appears inwardly as the ultimate consciousness. It is the highest state we can reach through our ego while remaining egoistic in our approach to life. Each religion has its way of explaining this. As the self-as-ego diminishes and the self-as-soul is enhanced, we increasingly experience ourselves as innately one with everything and everyone.

In the Native American culture, the medicine wheel is an example of the archetypal level. The medicine wheel forms a symbolic geography that enables the individuals to orient themselves in the cosmic scheme. The alignment of a connection to place, spiritual and physical, is an essential aspect of our ability to balance our energy, awaken to ourselves, and orient ourselves to life. The four directions give us place while the animal spirits give us our power and kinship with our transcendental origins.

Our noetic capacity slumbers within the unconscious as an archetypal form, a soul genetic potential, awaiting our conscious awakening. As the noetic mind awakens, we will begin to see into our unconscious without the need to reflect its content symbolically and our dreams gain greater lucidity.

**Spiritual.** I placed the label on the ring with the archetypal simply because the spiritual permeates everything, while at the "membrane" with the archetypal it formulates a mirror or a nexus, depending on awareness of the individual. The spiritual reflects and responds to the balance and alignment of all the levels. In this level, the balancing energy acts as wholeness. It moves through the chakras and levels as a process of breathing.

Each of the other levels provides a conduit for spiritual energy. As the noetic becomes balanced, aligned, and strengthened, the spiritual level becomes more evident. It reflects our transcendent nature into our psychological, social, and physical realities.

The spiritual level is hard to articulate except through shared experiences or stories that reflect actual experiences of spiritual realities. For that reason, most religions rely on dogma or a set of beliefs or principles to anchor their faith. Our personal sense of spirit develops in a central way in our soul-space where we live as spirit and express and differentiate ourselves through the various levels.

The spiritual level of the aura becomes more apparent as we organize our personality and psychospiritual structure with soul as the conscious center of the way we perceive, think, feel, imagine, and act physically. The degree of our centering in ego or in soul reflects into the overall ambiance of the energy fields. Life-long learning is a personal *soul-journ*ey and an actualization of universal love. Soul-space is where we are aware and embody self as soul. We experience soul as the individual awareness of universal love.

## What imbalances the noetic field?

Noetic Field Balancing is powerful and direct. The inner dimensions of our psyche appears around our physical body as layers of beliefs, emotions, and archetypal forms. Our issues and concerns appear as blocks and distortions in the energy patterns of this field. The blocks and distortions are caused by physical and emotional trauma, self judgment and limiting beliefs, or from external psychic pressures from individuals, groups or institutional belief systems. The blocks and distortions affect the containment and movement of energy within our consciousness, and may result in psychological problems or physical disease. The indiscriminate use of recreational drugs or alcohol can severely damage the noetic field.

Blocks are an attempt to protect. As such, they become integrated into the sustaining structure of our personality. As we create meaning in response to trauma, we adapt to that meaning as if it were normal. Thus, the trauma, and the resulting meaning that we construct, become normalized. We adapt to the level of our injury, and then believe that is who we are. Consequently, as we become more centered through balancing, our sense of self shifts from ego to soul.

While our ego adapts to trauma, our soul continues to pursue transformation. In the deepest sense, our field is out of balance as one phase in a process caused by our drive to awaken spiritually and transform the quality of our lives and our experience. In a more conventional sense, any concern, trauma, or issue that brings us to counseling, or requires therapy, reflects in our field as an imbalance.

Through prayer and focus, an altered state of consciousness unfolds, enabling the practitioner to engage the blocks and distortions directly in the energy field. Through this spiritual rapport, the practitioner is able to assist us to transform and balance our consciousness. Transformation occurs through an alliance of intervening spiritual energies, unfolding soul energies, and our own self forgiveness.

## Why balance?

When our field is out of balance, so is our perception of and connection with life. Because imbalance and weakness appear in the field before it manifests in the physical body, balancing can be a preventive physical therapy, as well as, therapy for the transformation of emotional and mental issues. By understanding the noetic field and directly engaging its distortion, we can transform the blocked energy created by trauma, choice, socialization, and daily challenges.

These sessions provide a powerful support, strengthening our alignment, center, clarity, and well being. It is an effective complement to therapy and healing, and promotes our spiritual progress. The effects of therapeutic balancing are often subtle, and at other times, very dramatic. The results of the session can range from deep relaxation, and perceptual clarity, greater spiritual alignment, or enlightenment. When the field is balanced, it is fluid, smooth, and energized, resuming its natural function of nourishing the body, protecting the psyche, and integrating the body, mind, soul, and spirit. We may experience an expansive sense of well-being, greater enthusiasm, heart-felt presence, ease in daily living, more joy, or peace. More importantly, Noetic Field Balancing strengthens our connection and awareness of the spiritual centrality of our nature: our self as energy and Holiness. To realize this is to know the true nature of reality.

## HISTORY

I developed Noetic Field Balancing from my experience as a student at Quimby Center, thirty-five years of clinical experience, and academic work as founder and president of Southwestern College. The basis for Noetic Field Balancing evolved out of the technique of aura balancing. Dr. Neva Dell Hunter, founder of Quimby Center, developed aura balancing from the healing work of Phineus Parkhurts Quimby and material gained through her inspirational work with John-Clark McDougall. Quimby was an American Transcendentalist who developed a form of spiritual healing in the mid-1800's that he called the "Science of the Christ." I met Dr. Hunter in 1967 through a mutual friend, Muriel Engle. I had dropped my classes during my senior year at the University of California, Santa Barbara, because I was experiencing a great deal of inner pressure, a lack of direction, and an inability to study.

At the time of our meeting, Dr Hunter explained that aura balancing is a form of spiritual therapy in which the practitioner works directly with the energy fields surrounding and penetrating the physical body. The practitioner approaches the self as energy and directly engages the psychological trauma, analogous to the way a surgeon physically touches an organ. In response to emotional disturbance, mental anguish, and spiritual imbalance, we make judgments, which create blocks that reflect in the fields of energy that surround us. With the help of the Light (as she called it), the practitioner assists by finding these blocks and leading us into self-forgiveness. It sounded good to me. I agreed to a session. At the time, my exploration of consciousness-oriented psychologies and spiritual experiences helped me trust the process.

The impact was dramatic. I experienced energy sensations and feelings moving in and around my physical body, and a mysterious resolution of my inner conflicts. Afterward, I felt clear, centered, and ready to complete my senior year.

## Apprentice to a Mystery

After graduation, I headed for Dr. Hunter's school in New Mexico. I was excited about this dramatic demonstration of therapy. Conventional therapies had seemed lacking, and aura balancing represented to me the missing link that joined my experiences, spiritual training, and academic studies into one model. I needed to discover how it worked. Later, I added the dimension of the *noetic field* as a means to further account for the role of consciousness, and to incorporate the *quantum* model as presented by David Bohm.

There, I met Ellavivian Power, who wrote the definitive book on aura balancing called the *Auric Mirror,* and Stephen Broscoff who developed a body-centered approach. As an apprentice and colleague, I worked and lived with this team from 1968 until Dr. Hunter's death in 1978. After this time, my approach to balancing was influenced by my study and practice of "soul transcendence," with John-Roger Hinkin. John-Roger, founder of the Church of the Movement of Spiritual Inner Awareness (MSIA), adapted aura balancing to work with a spiritual consciousness that he called the "Mystical Traveler."

The greatest blessing is the deepening and softening of my heart and the wisdom that is conveyed to me with each person with whom I work. I am able to present myself to the Holy Spirit and to the service of souls in a way that promotes spiritual progression, health, happiness, well-being, and healing. I believe my role is to be a spiritual enabler, guide, or tutor. I am able to gently suggest and draw out the client's inherent wisdom. When all goes well, I am able to help them remember and touch the reality that they are originally and inherently divine. In a sense, I am an educator who can enhance the student's *soul-astic* achievement. When our souls touch, we awaken more to the immensity of spirit.

The following discussion requires a more specialized education, than the scope of this writing; however, it offers a perspective of energy balancing that encompasses our potential. I discuss the technique at length in: *Eyes Made of Soul: The Theory and Practice of Noetic Field Therapy.* Later in this chapter, I will present some techniques for balancing that can be readily applied within the context of our current course of study.

## BALANCING THE NOETIC FIELD

Noetic Field Balancing requires the practitioner to surrender to the highest spiritual source possible. As I teach this, it is an alignment with the Father-Mother God through the Christ (Jesus Christ if you prefer). Certainly, this is the Christ as a mystical force, a transcendent and present being, and the Holy Spirit. Therefore, just as accessible through Allah the Merciful, or for that matter, any deep alignment with source. In my experience, the deeper the alignment, the greater the results.

During my many years of practice, people from many spiritual backgrounds have come for sessions with me. The differences were never an obstacle. With true spiritually there is never a conflict. The conflict comes from the dogmatic evolution of a given teaching or teacher. The earth-based *goddess,* the Buddhists *beingness* and quest for *Buddahood,* The Native American *Great Spirit,* the Jewish *Yahweh,* the Taoist *Tao,* the Muslim *Allah,* to name a few, are complementary ways of engaging *universal holiness.* I am not saying they are the same. I am saying there is no conflict between any true spiritual alignment. Even this mystical Christianity, and awakening the "inner Christ," finds a place with more fundamentalist viewpoints. Within the sacred space created by this divine relationship, wondrous things can happen. Sometimes our expectations are met or surpassed. Other times, nothing appears to happen. That is the way of the Holy Spirit.

Spiritual work is non-adversarial and non-coercive. True spirituality embraces the curriculum of our souls and honors our choices, regardless of how they may seem. Spirit will intervene only at our request. We also appear to be inherently linked to a divine plan or sacred matrix that perpetually prompts us to seek wholeness, fulfillment, peace, loving, joy, and home.

In our ego, we want to do life separate from God. Transformation requires that we choose to do it with God, which is the essence of self-forgiveness. Because we have created a backlog of actions based on separation from self (dualistic mind-set), grace may not appear immediately evident in our forgiveness.

Within this context, an altered state of consciousness is created in which the higher sense perception (HSP) of the practitioner and the client is enhanced. Angels, spiritual guides, and numerous holy forces may participate in serving and healing the client. Through HSP, the practitioner discerns blocks and may perceive information about the nature, cause, and judgment associated with imbalance. Coaching more and telling less is more efficient, effective, and healthier for the client.

## Preparing the Client

When a client makes an appointment, the practitioner talks about the need to be accepting and that one's own desires for greater health, well-being, and happiness are sufficient preparation. Abstaining from the use of recreational drugs two weeks before and abstaining from moderate alcohol use the day before can also help. If there is drug or alcohol abuse, a longer time of abstinence may be needed. Since this is a spiritual approach, no promises are made as to results. We all have areas of mental and emotional disturbance that we have forgotten. Greater alignment and understanding of our spirituality and purpose is an innate drive. We adapt to our forgotten hurts and judgment. Clients are often surprised at how different they feel after they are balanced. Some things are easy to change. Other areas may need more time or prolonged counseling before we are ready to balance them. Noetic Field Balancing is an effective complement to any process of physical or psychological healing and can dramatically facilitate that process. Though miracles can happen, this service is not meant to replace needed medical, psychiatric, or other therapeutic needs.

## Preliminary Steps

First the practitioner orients the client to the nature of the balancing. The client reclines, face up, on a massage table or couch. The practitioner stands. The reclining position of the client is relaxing while providing the practitioner easy access to the field. The physical and emotional balancing is done silently. If a question or observation comes up, the client is encouraged to speak. During the mental-spiritual balancing, focus statements help the client discover and clarify beliefs, and to facilitate self-forgiveness. Jewelry, metal, and shoes might affect the balancing process, so they are removed.

## Prayer

With the client relaxing, I begin with a prayer that goes something like this:

*Father-Mother God, I just now ask to be surrounded by the light of the Christ and, through the Holy spirit, I ask for only that which is to the highest good of all concerned, keeping in mind the destinies on the planet. Through the permission of the Christ and the guidance of the Holy Spirit, I also ask that any angels, beings of light, or teachers who wish to be here and assist for the well-being of all concerned also be granted. We ask for this in perfect love and perfect understanding, and we thank you for this time. Thy will be done.*

At this point I may have insights into the consciousness of the client. Engaging the Christ as a spiritual form complements all ways of life and teachings that pursue unconditional loving. Regardless of spiritual heritage, the balancing strengthens the client's particular spiritual practice.

This is not the only prayer that can be used. The opening prayer will always contain certain universal elements that translate into any truly spiritual tradition. The prayer includes an:

- invitation for an alignment with and surrender to a higher power,

- admonition of impeccability,

- sanctification of the place,

- dedication to the highest good, and

- expression of gratitude.

## Opening and Balancing

After the prayer, I use a crystal pendulum to open the energy field at the solar plexus. The pendulum is an instrument of focus for me and a means of engaging the subtle level of the energy patterns. This focus creates a nexus through which distorted patterns can deconstruct, soul forms unfold, and through which spiritual energy can be transmitted. The permission of the client, the alignment with spirit, and my intention form the focus through the pendulum that opens the energy field. In some cases this focus can be provided by touch, or mental acuity. Since my intention is to serve the Holiness of the client and the Universe, the actual spiritual event of balancing is governed by the Holy Spirit, or Nous.

As the pendulum is introduced, I sense the subtle changes that occur. Usually the field engages and begins to open just above the solar plexus. When this occurs, the pendulum gently begins to rotate. When the aura is open, the pendulum stops. I approach each imbalance in a similar way. This action creates a high level of rapport with the client. It also makes the sensitive levels of the client extremely vulnerable, which, combined with the loving presence, invites a deep level of transformation.

The protective energy fields interface with the psychospiritual environment. Blocks are beliefs or judgments that have been integrated into the sustaining structure of the individual. As such, the basic self will protect the status quo by regarding such beliefs as truth and sustain them until directed otherwise. Therefore, the individual must authorize any changes to this structure. The client's vulnerability facilitates access to original choices and judgments that formed the imbalancing belief, and to the soul intentions that involved the client in the particular circumstance.

Next, I scan the field with my hand to first increase attunement and then to find the blocks and distortions. My hands are trained to see and sense. The impressions are processed through the nervous system and brain like any other stimulation and translated into meaning. Because my subtle body is awake, movement in the energy field registers like physical sensation. This is true for most of us. We have trained ourselves to focus away from these impressions because of social and psychological influences. In this phase of the balancing, talking is not necessary, except perhaps to help the client relax. The client may feel subtle movements of energy, feeling, emotion, or images.

When I find a block or distortion, I use the pendulum to engage the energy. When the pendulum rotates, it reflects the transformation of energy in the field. I proceed in this manner until all the areas are balanced.

A natural guidance leads from one step to the next. Balancing the physical and emotional energy fields is often done silently. I may ask the client what she or he is experiencing or suggest a deep breath. Facilitative talking is always needed in the mental-spiritual balancing because the client needs to discover and clarify his or her beliefs in order to provide the clarity and the precision necessary for effective self forgiveness.

129

Blocks are symbolic in nature. As such, they may correspond to any dimension of the self from the physical body through the etheric, or to any one of the spiritual centers, or chakras. The blocks appear in the field at distances from the body that correspond to their depth in the psyche. Beginning closest to the physical body, the levels are: physical, imaginal, emotional, mental, archetypal. The personal energy of the field extends approximately an arms length.

At some point toward the end, the client turns over so that I can check the field from the back. The balancing continues until the entire field is smooth and silky. Before finishing, the client once again turns face up.

## Closing

When the balancing appears to be complete, the client is asked if there is anything else. When nothing more presents itself, the client releases all concerns into higher consciousness. I proceed to close the field with intention and the blessing of the Holy Spirit.

This entire process usually takes from forty-five minutes to one hour, or occasionally longer. The client's immediate experience may be as subtle as feeling more peaceful or as dramatic as experiencing bliss, greater clarity or transformation. The balancing process continues for three days after the actual session has ended. During this time, the client completes any processing and adapts to any changes. This period of adjustment provides a new base line upon which the subconscious can regulate the psyche. For that reason, it is recommended that the client abstain from alcohol, recreational drug use, and sex for those three days. Alcohol and drugs may disrupt the transformative changes and disperse the new organization of energy. Sexual intimacy is very powerful and, until the changes stabilize, may be confusing on a subtle level. Recreational drugs always act against the balancing process and should not be used when developing a strong, aligned, balanced aura.

It is recommend that clients take life as it comes for the following three days, and not analyze or worry about their experience. Journaling and reflective insights are often helpful. Changes are often deep and can be accompanied by uncomfortable symptoms such as minor flu or restlessness. On the other hand, the client may experience a great peace or joy. In any case, by the end of the three days, the client will have adjusted to the changes and have a new sense of what is normal. With each session, the client becomes more and more skillful in using the balancing session and maintaining and promoting balance in general. Each session provides a stronger platform for the next session. For that reason, three initial sessions are recommended. These sessions should be at least two weeks apart, however, a longer spacing is fine. After the first three sessions, a touch-up every six to twelve months is recommended. (Practitioners of this technique can be found on the web-site: http://mystery-school.com.)

## APPLICATION

Balancing the noetic field in its simplest form is an application of living. Spirit, as it actualizes through form, is the unfolding of spirit into life. When we make a choice or take action spirit meets us. Simply going for a walk begins to balance us. Often by calling on our holiness, or some form of alignment with our higher selves and honoring our limiting choice or disturbing situation, we move to a greater balance. Higher consciousness must be asked. It will not inflict. As we resolve our experience, we empower our vertical center. In the following are some ways to balance ourselves and to assist others, within the scope of what we have learned so far. The technique just described as Noetic Field Balancing, requires more extensive training. These techniques are very powerful and need to be approach with care and respect.

### Looking at Hands

1.  Through a prayer, ask to be surrounded by the Light for the highest good.

2.  Look at the palms of your hands, and relax allowing the reflective relationship to generate energy.

3.  Reflect on the situation, circumstance or issue that is causing you concern. Forgive yourself for judging yourself. If you are aware of a specific judgment like, "I am no good because I failed." Forgive yourself for that belief.

4.  Take a deep breath and let go. Proceed to the next circumstance or awareness of judgment.

The *hand pendulum* technique is a more complex variation of *looking at hands*. The pendulum is an effective focus for noetic balancing, and is safe when used in the technique described. For this technique only, hold the pendulum in one hand over the palm of the other hand.

1.     Through a prayer, ask to be surrounded by the Light for the highest good.

2.     First practice using the pendulum. Hold the pendulum in one hand suspended over the palm of the other hand. Practice allowing the pendulum to spin clockwise. This is a convention of balancing energy in your field. It may spin counter-clockwise. Visualize it spinning clockwise. At this point we are practicing a convention that means the same thing to your basic self and high self (see chapter on Huna). A clockwise spin means balancing is occurring and when it stops the balancing of that focus is complete.

3.     After calling in the Light and practicing, you are ready to begin. Hold the pendulum over your palm, call your holiness forward and ask for connection with your high self.

4.     See your body in a sphere of Light. Next, scan your body with the focus of your attention. As your attention finds an area that needs balancing, the pendulum will spin clockwise. As it does let go and relax, allow the light to do the work. If judgments appear, forgive yourself. When the rotation stops, scan for another point by directing your focus to other areas of your body or in the field around your body. You can start with areas of tension or discomfort, then scanning less apparent locations.

5.     After you have moved through the physical body, scan around your body. The pendulum will spin clockwise, reflecting that there is an area that needs balancing, and that balancing has begun. Again, as images or feelings arise, be aware of your judgments, limiting beliefs, or the incident in which the choice or judgment was made, and forgive yourself. When the pendulum stops, move on.

6.	Proceed in this way until there is no more movement. This will indicate you have done as much as you can with this technique. A balancing by a qualified practitioner will go further. Bless yourself. Place yourself, situations and relationships, hopes and dreams in the Light, take a deep breath and release. There is always a higher consciousness that is guiding your process.

## Partner Focusing

For this method, sit opposite a partner. You will be taking turns being the facilitator or client role, using the Structural Symbolic Focusing Protocol from the chapter on Noetic Psychology (page 107).

1.	Call in the Light to surround both of you for the highest good.

2.	The practitioner role will be a witness and make the focus statements from the protocol. For example, ask: "Share a time when you experienced being alone, afraid, powerless or hurt." The statement is sufficient, the practitioner must avoid any attempt to coach, counsel, or process. If your partner appears stuck, only repeat the statement. The client role says whatever comes to mind while the facilitator role listens with a reductive focus and says nothing. Maintaining eye contact is very helpful. After each step, both take a deep breath, and remain silent for a suitable length of time. Maintain eye contact, and ask if another time comes to mind. If not, proceed to the next statement. The client forgives self for any judgments or limiting beliefs.

3.	When all of the statements are complete, change roles and repeat the process.

4.	When both are done, take a moment to place everything and each other into the Light, maintain a moment of silent eye contact, and then thank each other.

## Hand Scan Balancing

In this method, we will directly engage the energy field of another person with our hands. When aligned with higher consciousness, touching a block will promote balance. Again, we will use a practitioner and client role. The practitioner must proceed without any agenda for the client, or his or her own importance. This technique can be used as a stand alone, or after a counseling session or conversation in which an associate shared some concern or difficulty. It is not a "fix-someone" or "be-important" technique. Be respectful, loving and cautious.

1.  The client role sits in a chair and the practitioner stands. Placing hands on the client's shoulders or over his/her head, palms toward the client, call in the Light for the highest good.

2.  Place one hand over the top of the client's head. Do not touch the body. Use the other hand to scan the energy field. As you feel or sense something hold your hand at that spot. You may feel movement. Hold your hand on that spot until it seems as if the balancing has occurred. You can switch hands for convenience of reach, or place your hands on opposite sides of the clients body. Cross over the shoulders or head for a few moments, asking again that the Light serve the client for the highest good. When you sense completion, you are done. One way you may sense completion is that you are unable to find any more locations upon which you can work. Another way is that the energy field will become smooth. You may feel a sense of well being and expanded energy. The person in the client role may feel blissful, centered and relaxed.

3.  Change roles and complete the same process.

## A PASSAGE INTO DAY

By engaging the healing energies of life through Noetic Field Balancing, we open new doors to our spiritual understanding and graceful living. This offers a point of departure for exploring a larger perspective of human reality and the implications that it holds for our well-being. We are wondrous even in our most challenged moments. Ralph Waldo Emerson believed that we had within us all the wisdom of nature and the universe. If that is so, our injuries foretell our healing and our limitations foretell our expansiveness. In this universe of energy, consider that therapy is a place where souls meet and impersonal intimacy reclaims its forgotten selves until all exists in a sea of loving.

*When we meet*
*in the heart of the creator,*
*our wounds*
*become a warrior's footprint,*
*our trials and tribulations*
*become a healing balm,*
*our dark night,*
*a passage into day.*

Our evolving mastery unfolds a deeper relationship to self and spirit. In the teachings of Hermes and Pythagorus, we find kindred spirits, offering access to the mystery. We find keys to the formation of the universe and our humanity, as a microcosm, an "image and likeness." They offer an invitation to join a lineage that began with the first breath, unfolding into the present creation. This lineage culminates in Jesus the Christ, who fully awakened as the Christ within the physical form. This changed us. The potential of our holiness activates our genetic possibility. Though it is not clearly apparent, we live in a new day and new dawn, and our witness a planetary re-birth. As we choose a new baseline, we become conscious agents of this transformation. The foot prints of eternity become many.

# REFERENCES

Waterman, R D. *Through The Eyes of Soul: The Theory and Practice of Noetic Field Therapy.* RDW, 1999.

# Chapter Seven

# FABRIC OF SELF

When we peel back all of the layers, we find an ancient soul fulfilling an archetypal impulse to explore, love, live, and create. We do this with the ultimate intent of actualizing ourselves as the individual experience of universal holiness. This *sense of self* is the ultimate intimacy of macro- and microcosm. Unlike the "lilies of the field," birds of the air, animals of the forest and field, we have the ability to trap our essence in belief, though we yearn for the freedom of direct understanding through direct experience. Yet, beliefs enable us to focus on discrete aspects of experience. We choose the world of our experience through the beliefs that we create. That is the key to our success, and our consternation. There is a covenant written in our souls that says we can retrieve ourselves from any reality we choose by remembering that we are Divine. However, we are finally able to remember that we have believed that we are belief and forgotten that we are divine. That is the key that locks and unlocks the door. This is the method by which we coalesce experience as soul-wisdom. We are the *foot prints of eternity*. Foot prints one day wash away or blow in the wind and forget the imprint that they held. So, we must remember our eternity. Regardless, the wind will take us and sea will receive us, but we may not remember the journey, because we did not save any of our experience for the journey home.

In Chapter one, we explored perception as a technology of making reality. Our understanding is more than a lens through which we make sense of life, it is co-creative. It is the other side of the looking glass. Perception is how life knows how to see us. In quantum terms, the elemental particles of life have several possible manifestations until something interacts with them. Our interaction chooses the reality. We explored how our beliefs shape what we see and how we are met. Our beliefs modify the fabric of self. For good or ill, the seamless flow of light and life must conform to our jurisdiction. We often suffer until we realize that it is ourselves that set the boundary, and it was our co-conspiracy that brought us to our current world. So, our choice is co-conspirator vs. co-creator. At some point, self as *foot print*, becomes self as *face print*. The metaphor of religious admonitions play upon the vibratory strings of self. We are the "image and likeness." We are the "word become flesh." As our beliefs become congruent with our imperative, the fabric of our DNA conjoins the archetypal geometry as a garment of light that the ancients call the body of light, chariot, the Mer Ka Vah. As we loosen the sedimentation of limiting self beliefs, our holiness ignites. The dark night is a loss of an ego based on external admonitions. The tethers that tie us to external descriptors wear thin. Our psychology takes its shape from the holiness within us. The body follows the lead, the cellular adaption, in the quest for survival, drops it conformity, and initiates its sleeping allegiance to the deeper imperative of its sacred geometry, of its longing, of its soul, of its remembrance of home.

In Chapter Two, we embraced the learning moment. The *noegenesis* of apprehending new understanding directly from experience. Life is a rhythm of learning: of formation and transformation. By embracing this heuristic cycle through bracketing, deconstruction and epiphany, the soul and God reveal their truth through the vortex of being present. In the presence of nothing, truth unfolds in the void of the deconstructed *print*, between the previous *step* and the next *step*. The *footprint* is indexed to the intentionality that invited it to impress itself on the surface of life: *noesis* and *noema* walking itself through eternity.

When I work with someone, or want to understand, I use this natural flow of reality to inform me. I engage and bracket the noema and in the deconstruction, I ride the current of reality and truth reveals itself to me as impressions, sensations, and pictures. Recent and ancient events unfold as images, symbol and metaphor. At times, I am still and the flow moves across the receptors of my internal sensorium of eyes, ears, and dimensional surfaces. Time is a circumference that approaches the still-point of knowing. At other times, I am riding the currents of the time line. The enfolding and unfolding *hollomovement* washes its artifacts upon the beaches of my soul. Form is the effect of soul interfacing with its currently compatible reality. I learn to see myself and others by the impressions we make on life, our *foot prints*. Life and firmament gives us what we want. As we learn to choose well, our *foot prints* become more like eternity, but not the same. *Foot prints* make impression and are only momentarily impressive.

In holographic projection, we see the image because information is projected on a matrix of light. In Chapter three, models of consciousness help us understand phenomenon through the structure of form. Structure is the dynamic of how content relates. What are the functions of the three selves, levels of consciousness, and chakras. Sacred geometry is implicit in spiritual anatomy. Our reality flows in and around us as a function of the soul. Ego sustains itself through its many faceted reflection on the surface of life, while soul is an incarnation of the Logo. Our actualization brings us to the mastery of being in this world and not of this world. This takes us to Chapter four and the Journey of the Soul.

While our geometry unfolds upon the time line, our soul incarnates into our developing form. The organism is receptive to its expanding matrix. Our intention unfolds reflexively through events as we fulfill the curriculum of our soul as destiny. Fulfillment is an internal event. The outer glory is in service to the inner event. It is the attainment of self that is made possible by the journey. We are the promise.

In Chapter Five, we embrace an integral psychology as an actualizing organism, responding to the call to self. Psychological issues are stepping stones to the realization of self. Issues reflect reversals in our field of consciousness caused by beliefs that trap our awareness into perspectives that imitate truth, yet are separating constructs from self, soul and holiness. The remedy is in the deconstruction of separative and distorting beliefs, this act frees the actualizing health of the soul's agenda. To be congruent with self is to embrace health, fulfillment and grace. The catalyst is the therapeutic witness of the practitioner.

In Chapter Six, we consider the deeper nature of the field itself as energy. We embrace all as energy, as the texture of life, of space. We engage space itself as an entity, a living field. As we reach out and engage the texture of this field, we follow its contours into the intimacy of conscious, of noetic field. Holiness is present. It is in us and all around us. Nested within this cosmic form are all the dimensional variances of the One. Our geometric center is the alignment of body, light body and soul. With each physical breath, there is a cosmic breath. It is the yoga of infinity. We populate our space with our practice realities. These constellated beliefs limit and oppose our center, or enhance and expand the life field from our center. The unconscious that is the mythical receptacle of our issues emerges as the field surrounding our body. We can grasp the contours of perception and adjust the lens directly. The key is our willingness to choose self as the primary instrument of understanding. Our physical body is a sensory interface between the worlds that enables us to learn and apply the science of the Soul in increments that make sense to our noetic infancy.

139

# PARADIGM SELF

The ancient admonition to "know thyself" is as appropriate and sweet today as it was in ancient times. The key to fulfilling our lives is to solve the mystery of self. We must extract our sense of self from the mirror and look inward to the radiant life of soul. The ultimate solution to all symptoms lies in the self as a spiritual transformation. Of the therapist, even more rigor is expected. The effectiveness of the therapist correlates to their alignment, integration and comfort with their own holiness. Are we courageous enough to be whole? You might say, "of course." Then, on more self-observation, you discover that much of your actions are dedicated to preserving the status quo. What is this status quo? It is always what your basic self believes it to be. It is a function of your survival, safety, nurture, shelter, and power needs. It is a synthesis of how you see yourself in the world and how the world sees you. It is your active paradigm. The more it is constructed from fear and the protection of inadequacies, the more forceful and clever is the protection. This protection is subtle and automatic, so if we do not train ourselves to observe it, we will not understand that we are doing it. This is the ego and ultimately it will dissolve into our soul. This is not good or bad. We must at some point make the choice conscious concerning what to perpetuate and what aspect we would prefer to discontinue. Symptoms of defending the status quo are:

- arguing a position

- irrational anger

- "yah, but" phrases

- narrow intellectual inquiry

- mentalizing

- rationalizing

- explaining

- embarrassment

140

- making excuses

I debated whether to call this discussion the *status quo self* or the *paradigm self.* The challenge of this self in therapy is pervasive. We are continually tempted to want to maintain the status quo and simultaneously seek enlightenment. I began to see a pattern when working with individuals who appeared to be highly motivated toward transformation. Despite their best, or stated, intention, they responded in a way that took us away from the point rather than toward it. The more obvious were "yah but," change of subject, or rationalizing. Instead of tracking the transformational patterns, we mysteriously found ourselves "fencing" with nuances of meaning or abstractions. Decoys abounded. When we are centered, we have little need to promote our position or fortify our self esteem. The paradigm self includes self-concept and more. It is a cosmology. A world view. We live in the center of our universe and feel safe, supported and comforted by it. We are enfolded in an archetype that, to our basic self, is true, is reality.

Anchored in the basic self, the paradigm self constellates our phenomenal universe. From the perspective of the Basic Self, we believe this is the universe that gives us life and breath and if something happens to it, we believe we will die. The paradigm self does not need to change for us to progress. It does need an adjustment in status. When we center in the paradigm self, we use life to reassure and reinforce our traditional reality. The ego becomes subtle. Rudolf Steiner called this subtlety the "spirits of assuras." Energized by high archetypal forces, our paradigm is self-evident and electric. We all have style, yet that is all that it is: style without substance.

Our fantasies and projections are attempts to make reality conform to our personal paradigm, and their ruminations, conversations, and actions serve to preserve the status quo. We agree on our reality, and perception negotiates the reality that we believe is so. We imbue life with our concept of it. Of course, it has its own nature. Nature evolves through our understanding of it. Just as our nature evolves through our understanding of ourselves.

Our impulse to discover and understand must work in concert with our need to feel safe and survive. We must accommodate both forces. I am continually amazed at my tendency to protect my world view, while my goal is always to discover truth. It is much like driving a car with one foot on the gas and one on the break, applying pressure simultaneously. I am embarrassed when I make a mistake. I become defensive, even if it is only for a moment, when someone challenges my favorite truth. So, I challenge myself. Does my discovery serve to preserve the status quo of my imposter self, or, to liberate my perception so I can discover the deeper true-self? The balance to the *paradigm-self* is the *centering-self*.

# CENTERING

Centering is not abstract. It is literally a conduit of light that aligns our body, emotions, minds, intentionality, and soul. When we are present in this alignment, we enfold our awareness into a spiritual dimension, while remaining engaged in the physical and psychic environment that surrounds us. When we center, we activate a force-field of love, power and truth.

We live in a time of inner and outer transitions. These transitions accelerate the pace and magnitude of experience. In transition, our reference for self continually changes. Our externally acquired references become unreliable. Old, reliable references for stability and well-being no longer serve to give us our sense of place, direction, or continuity. Our addictions and co-dependence, as well, appear less reliable. While transitions reveal the *face of the imposter*, centering reveals truth.

When we center, our hearts expand, while the sedimentation of ego transforms. Developing a greater access to *center* strengthens our direct relationship to our inherent love, intelligence, power and truth. When we are centered, we experience an assurance, or solidity, about life, regardless of circumstances. We are more resilient. Center aligns us with the inner matrix of our humanity, providing a beacon of continuity irregardless of how formidable the transition may become. Chaos reinforces center.

This inner matrix is a holy place. The challenges and antics of life may circle around us – cajoling, enticing, coercing – yet lose their grasp on claiming or shaping us, or causing us to abandon our purposes and adopt theirs. In contrast to having our attitude and perception shaped by our ego-states, mental confusion or emotional chaos, we become the center pole. Extending our center further orients our sense-of-self to our innate holiness and forms a stronger connection to the truth that is earth, place, universe, and transcendence. Our status quo may attempted to bypass our conscious intent to preserve our traditional conditioning. As the basic self gains a feeling of the two tracks, we are able to direct our instinctual alignment to form an allegiance to the *soul-*

*story,* and re-form the *ego-story* to its natural service function, such as *middle management.*

In centering, the intention is always love and wholeness. When we create from center, there is no shadow in the manifestation, no shadow of unintended consequence. As our centers coalesce, the one center ignites and a new standard of life quickens in the hearts of the many. We are the answer we have been looking for. We are the promise.

## TRACKING OUR LIVES

On one track, we travel as ego, self concept, the self as belief. We build ego from our mental and emotional response to life. Its demands, challenges, social mores, and environmental forces dominate our perception of who we are. We define ourselves through the eyes of others and "society." When we look at life as metaphor, our soul's journey reveals itself in each moment. When we are present, in a consciousness of noegenesis, the present story is the soul's story. We are tracking the soul's journey as it evolves and transforms through the episodic curriculum of our lives.

On the second track, soul is the eternal self made of spirit, and the substances that we refine and distill from life experience. Eons in the development, the soul is here to gain experience and fulfill ancient yearnings. As we learn to center and access our higher selves, soul expands into the daily activities of our lives. We increasingly feel secure in our participation in life.

Through ego and self-concept, we cling to a sense of continuity based on our story and the addictive emotions that stimulate our sense of being alive and important. Our evolution increasingly indexes our sense of continuity to our soul. Our mastery is an expression of riding both tracks: living in this world and meeting its challenges, while centering in soul.

### Structation

*Structation* is a word coined by the physicist David Bohm as a means of describing how form occurs in terms of quantum reality. We are reminded of Edmund Hursserl's structure of phenomenon. Beliefs and events are caused "non-locally" by intentionality. Intentionality emerges from center. Strong beliefs and a self-satisfied ego also behave and exert power as if they are center. Truth resonates in our center, while un-truth

143

promotes itself as the center – as an imposter center, which makes us prone to the influence of imposter forces. When our basic self is charged with preserving a status-quo that is replete with distorted beliefs in the form of dysfunctional and traumatic issues, centering is very difficult. The remedy is to re-structure our *self* paradigm. We can do this through gaining greater access to the our soul track by transforming the structure of our experience and by improving our nexus with higher consciousness.

The basic drive of the soul is to gain experience. For the most part, good or bad is the same to the soul. We prefer the grace and fulfillment that comes with living congruent lives, so we increasingly choose grace-fulfilling actions. When our action, thinking, and feeling are resonant with our soul's truth or intention, we are congruent. On the physical level, we like to be healthy, have well-being and experience pleasure. These are powerful influences from which we learn choice, and, ultimately, choose grace, well-being and fulfillment. The soul will only integrate experience that is fulfilled in grace. Incomplete patterns are recycled through our life experience until they are resolved.

Self concept is a gestalt of our belief system. This organization is based on a deeper archetypal pattern. We use the archetypal pattern as template for the formation of our personality. The archetype pre-disposes and the belief disposes. In both cases, these are acquired. There are deeper primordial formations that guide this process; however, the current focus is on those limiting beliefs and archetypes that we know we must de-construct in order to free the actualizing forces of the soul's intentionality.

As a symbolic means of accessing the unconscious, we employ various devices such as astrology, numerology, symbols, enneagram, personality types, etc., in order to find an orientation. These approaches are tools. They give our minds a way to identify our archetypal variations. "Oh," we realize, "it wasn't personal. That is just the way we are." Our tendency is to act as if archetypes are the whole picture. We then create belief systems based on these abstractions. Once that happens, we set up the system as a perceptive lens that determines how we see life. The same thing happens to the teachings of enlightened masters. The teaching is originally of a high level when drawn from the clarity of the original master's statement. As the descendants re-interpret based on their agendas and limited grasp of these concepts, belief systems replace the truth, and the direct experience of the teaching. The teaching, at this point, is highly susceptible to being incorporated into political or religious power agendas, such as occurred at the Council of

Nicea in 325 AD. In this sense any archetypal or belief system shapes our perception, thus limiting our awareness of all that is occurring. By discovering and de-constructing these systems, we are better able to meet realty as it presents itself.

The following diagrams depict beliefs that block the actualization of soul intentionality. In this case, we are exploring abundance and worth as one vector and right relationship as another vector. Recalling Husserl's model of phenomenology, the beliefs in the diagram balloons are the *noema* and the arrows are the *noesis,* or intentionality. Our psychological issues are constellated belief systems. As we discover the beliefs that are structuring our life energy and perception in a way that blocks our actualization, we are in a position to deconstruct those beliefs, and, by doing so, free the actualizing force of the intentionality.

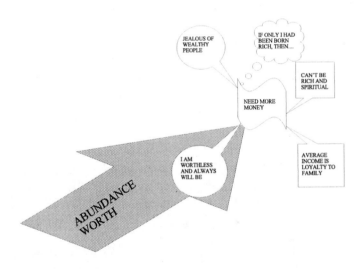

To arrive at these examples, we need to distill the key beliefs from our paradigm self, or status quo. In the following exercise, we will explore the relationship between the paradigm we live as a *status quo* and its relationship to the intentionality for which its is indexed. In *noegenesis,* we know directly from the present experience. For that to happen our perception must be structured in a way that allows for the noegenetic event. The purpose of the exercise is to map and distill the matrix of beliefs that structures the status quo. We can then deconstruct the overlay of beliefs systems and archetypal devices. The resulting

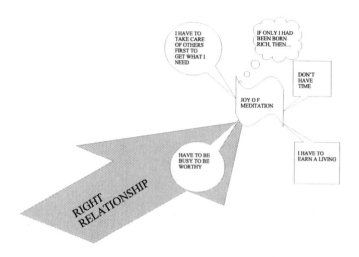

noegenesis is the experience of noesis. From the experience of noesis, we will be enable us to "structate" a reality that is in greater alignment with soul.

1.  Make a list of five beliefs, events, qualities, etc., that bring greater joy, love, or fulfillment.

2.  Make a list of five beliefs, events, qualities, etc., that are disturbing, based on trauma, unhappiness, or limiting beliefs.

3.  Each one of these events or beliefs is indexed to an intentionality. Choose one thing from either of the lists and apply this question. We then ask: what would my soul want to be, fulfill or gain by participating in this reality?

4.  If the item is positive, more than likely, the soul's intent was to have more of that or strengthen that. If it is negative, the intent might not at first be obvious. The universe brings us what we focus on. The soul seeks to fulfill itself, which it can only do by resolving all life issues in a way that adds more substance to itself. To integrate experience into the soul nature, it must be compatible with peace, love, joy, abundance, and enthusiasm. So, if the item is positive, the soul intent is indexed as the

motivation that gives it meaning. If it is negative, the item is indexed to a positive purpose that will result from resolving the seemingly negative experience. Diagram the intentionality that is indexed to the item you chose.

5.   Next, diagram the beliefs or choices that keep these items functioning in your status-quo. So, if the item you chose is positive, diagram all the beliefs and choices you make that keep you from receiving or doing this positive more often. If it is negative, diagram the beliefs, choices and behaviors that constellate this item.

6.   You now have the material to make a list of those beliefs and judgments that keep you from doing the positive action more often, and that keep your negative action solidly protected by your status-quo. In the greatest loving and kindness that you can manage, look at each belief and judgment and forgive yourself. Take a deep breath after each forgiveness.

7.   Repeat this protocol with each item on your list. It will work more powerfully if you proceed with a collaborator that helps you clarify and serve as a witness.

The evolution that we are promoting is one that refocuses our basic selves to use our soul-self as the reference for continuity and preservation. As long as our basic self believes that our story and the story of culture provides our continuity for self concept, survival, safety and nurture, our perception traps us in a realty that is limited and different from our truth.

## ACCESS

The true teaching occurs in the invisible fabric that is woven through our rapport. In this way, the *witness* reciprocally clarifies the intentional force of our soul-truth. In this way, the multidimensional energy can more easily unfold into our present conscious awareness, joining us, awakening in us, lifting, teaching, transforming. Holiness becomes our means of true communication. To accomplish these things, we need access, the keys to "heaven."

Our bodies are able to reflect awareness from all levels of consciousness. Once our bodies have an experience of any dimension, we can then reflect meaningful on that experience. Without that nexus, we have great difficulty orienting consciously to the subtleties of our greater consciousness. As long as our conditioning blocks our ability to feel what we are experiencing in our bodies, our sub-conscious, or basic self, does not know how to respond other than telling us that the response we are seeking has no reality for the present scope of our survival. To control and order society, individual awareness of the expanded self, must be blocked in some way. Religious history is based on a tradition of humanity being "asleep" to their higher nature in some way. Someone in that culture or tribe then has a transcendental experience and articulates his or her vision to that group. The vision is suppressed or embraced. If embraced, over time, the truth of that vision is increasingly replaced by politics, because successive generations cannot maintain the same level of connection. They carry too much "baggage" to participate in the reality of enlightenment, even though each person has the capacity to become enlightened.

I have been exploring noetic field balancing, as a therapeutic approach for over forty years. This is not a case of one year of experience repeated forty times. As my connection to Source deepens and my grasp of perception pushes into enlightenment, deeper causal levels of why we think like we do become apparent to me. There is something ancient in our genetics and collective unconscious that compels us to re-enforce our perception of duality and to accept conflict as the true and permanent state of our reality. Though we do not go into depth, in this writing, about the technique of *noetic field balancing,* we do practice the basics. One of the practices takes us to the understanding that beliefs are actual geometric structures that either distort or enhance our balanced and rhythmic exchange with the source of creation through our discrete soul nature. We can use our awareness to directly engage the issues of our clients in the unconscious energy field around our bodies. Access anchors transcendent consciousness into our bodies, enabling us to see past our illusions. As we do this, we can "see" into our subconscious and unconscious fields and, by so doing, respond to our clients on deeper levels. Access itself can resolve karmic forms in our field, clear reversals, and dissolve static energy.

Freud made us aware that our social and cultural mores caused us to suppress our basic drives. This suppression resulted in aberrant behaviors toward ourselves and others. Some of these behaviors were collectively condoned and some were not. Jung led us to a deeper view of causality. Great archetypal forces exist in the unconscious that shape the context in which we act and perceive reality. These are the unconscious gods and metaphysical deities of tribal rituals. Lucifer, Satan, and Jehovah are some of the archetypal forces in the Judeo-Christian tradition. Zues, Jupiter, and others preside in Greek antiquity. We could go on for pages, listing the equivalent discoveries of people around the globe. In short, Jung grouped all transcendental and extra-terrestrial forces into a band of archetypal forces and beings that have impact on humanity for good or ill. Then we must ask: "is good versus evil a reality, or does humanity have within its archetypal nature, and geometric programing, information that limits us from seeing the "bigger picture." For this reason, I think that wars and conflict are decoys that keep us distracted from discovering the true nature of ourselves and the workings of the universe. There may well be a conflict between "good and evil," but I am not so certain that any useful, or ultimate, answer exists within that paradigm. Having said that, I do consider that the "good/evil" paradigm does raise useful questions.

## Through the Looking Glass

I love this metaphor. When we look in a mirror, we see an image of our physical self that appears deceptively accurate. We unconsciously interact with this image, as if it is just fine. The first clue that we discover is that the image is reverse from left to right. A camera lens reverses the image from top to bottom. Not to say that this is not a helpful reality. Once we know the simple rule of perception, our way of looking at our image changes. The reality of reflective light is that this three dimensional physical reality is the one in which we play out the drama of our discovery and accomplishment, until we see beyond the "looking glass."

I love to teach. One of the main reasons is that each session is a new revelation. Recently, a student raised a concern. She loved her sense of liberation that came from realizing that she had based her value on her relationship to her husband and children, and that career had always been a secondary consideration. Forgiving herself for that belief was very powerful for her. She realized that the reason she embraced that life for so long was because that is the way she learned to know herself, that is how she learned to be "herself." Now, she was caught in the tragedy of "wasting all that time." She spontaneously transferred her "victimization" to a new level. She was angry all over again. My first

149

response was to continue to follow the energy and unfold the next self-forgiveness, or realization of a false belief. I stopped. My attention was drawn to a "space" on the left side of her head behind her ear. An implant? *Implants* increasingly appear during my sessions with clients. Implants are specialized geometric forms that lock perception into a specific viewpoint. We can understand implants in the context of Jung's archetypes and the collective unconscious. The difference being that noetic field therapy is progressing to a point in which the practitioner can detect subtler levels of the predisposing archetypes. In this case we went from an archetype of (1) *women find their meaning through men and motherhood* to (2) *as a women my definition is through being a victim,* to (3) *my power is in my self-righteousness and regret about my loss of time when I could have been free* (subtle victim). Rebelling against the archetype is a beginning. However, in the rebelling, one's self-concept continues to be determined by the archetype. Liberation remains illusive.

These implants can be cleared by witnessing and consciously naming them to the client, touching them and witnessing, pushing them out by anchoring unconditional love, or dissolving them with a projection of energy, or some combination. However, we need *access* to develop this level of sensitivity and skill. In this case, I told her to hold that thought, walked over to her and touch the implant. The higher spiritual energy of the alignment that I access dissolved it on contact. She took a deep breath and felt a freeing up through her head and chest. Her reality was instantly different. She experienced a sense of freedom and neutrality toward the great "crime against her womanhood." She was no longer perceptually locked into its imprint. Her identification with tragedy instantly became "her watching a movie about tragedy." The implant had locked her perception so that her fulfillment would always be limited by something. "Even if I am free now, I lost those years and can never compensate for them." The implant continued the limiting reality even though she had healed her personal judgments about herself. As long as the "implant" remained active, there would always be a predisposing force that re-constituted a victim paradigm, insuring the continued formation of victim beliefs. From my perspective our belief in conflict, or war, is similar.

Examples such as this are arising more frequently. I grew up with the image that spiritual reality was a divine conflict between good and evil. This was an overlay that was placed onto my experience as a way to make meaning. The nature of good and evil is illusive, and changeable as we change. Our attempt to determine rigid edicts seem to just polarize our reality even more. In our mythology, this war began when rebellious angels believed that they were the source and had no need to rely on anything greater than themselves. By so doing, they lost the awareness that they were larger than their circumstances, even the matrix of their morphogenic field. It seems to me this is the same metaphor through which we promote war.

We are always supported in our choice. That is the nature of unconditional love. However, there is a law of consequence. The a-priori movement of unconditional love contains a preference for us to return home, to fulfill our nature in love, grace and wholeness. Ah, the treacheries of free will. We forgot our Divine partnership. Our axis of power reversed, and we were no longer anchored in unconditional love, and with it, the loss of unlimited access to living energy. The Fall meant that we must dominate and take energy and resources from others in order to live, predisposing the ultimate rationalization of exploitive business practice and aggressive foreign policy. The commitment to this act decreed that our resources would be limited to that which was already invested in creation. That is, if we persisted. I concluded then that to engage in conflict, to win by being against, would ultimately create a lose/lose situation. Light battling dark would leave the winner with yet another source of energy. The shadow of this is that the new source, no mater how nobly won, was not renewable. The spoils of conquest, spoil. In a sense, the victor would already be dead.

I am convinced that we are in an end time and that we live in a world that is playing out ancient dramas. My client became neutral to the conflict with the removal of an implant (archetype) that she did not create. She may have allowed it or promoted it by falling out of her own grace, but that would have been millennia ago and so entangled with who did what to whom, that we may never find the release by digging for yet one more belief to forgive. Removing her implant changed her relationship to reality such that she was no longer in the "againstness game" of victim/victimizer. Her case is not a stand alone example. My conclusion is that "once upon a time" somebody discovered that they could create more resource by placing a program in the genetic morphogenic field of humanity that limited their perception, and that, by so doing, limited them to the realm of duality by controlling their perception. Once the mind is programed to perceive life and solutions through the lens of duality, that edict enfolds as science. Our highest ethic becomes *justice*. Grace must be "fair." There is nothing wrong with fairness, but when the standard is confined to local evidence, the non-local complement, that is the context of that event, remains illusive.

Some of us inherit this "gene" more than others. All of us have to break the spell.

Consider this: As we participate in the drama of this time, we seek grace, enlightenment, going home, spiritual power, and liberation. You name it. This sounds like a good thing. The market place is bustling. Who would consciously choose evil? Who would consciously choose to permanently be a "fallen angle?" By now, we should know that things are often not as they seem. What if, the cause of "light" against "dark," as played out in an adversarial format, is actually a turf war between two different organizations of "dark?" I suggest that there is an *imposter* running through all of this that cajoles the fundamentalist, new aggers, ascensionist and politicos all the same. Each group has its own "buzz" concerning these times. I have heard that many calamities have been averted that were prophesied because of the great "light work" that we have all done, and continue to do. Makes you feel good. Light work for one group is to conquer the "evil doers." To another group, it is activating your merkaba and jumping through a star gate. I think that there may be an aspect of truth to all of these. More simple, "light work" is discovering the holy place inside, and using that discovery to transform everything in our growing awareness that is unlike unconditional love. This is what I am calling access. The way I am framing this to myself, in terms of this writing, is that more people are choosing out of the practice of defining themselves as being the movie, and aligning with source as a witnesses to the movie. The drama plays on. Access helps us to be aware that we are not the movie.

The deception is more than our limiting beliefs. The deception is deeper into the geometry of our consciousness in a way that predisposes us to perceive and choose in terms of duality. What causes us to like limited and anti-Divine Self beliefs? Through sacred geometry, we can understand the spiritual physics that is the underpinning of noetic field balancing. As we include the deeper understanding of sacred geometry and spiritual physics in our balancing practice, we enter more directly into multidimensional aspects of the drama. As the potential for impact increases so does the subtlety of deception.

As my experience deepens, I look for helpful information in the market place. Briefly, the imposter techniques lock you into the wars of duality at an even deeper level than the implant I discussed earlier. I am not saying that duality is "bad" and wholeness is "good." I am saying that duality embedded in wholeness produces truly healing results. The mission of Noetic field balancing is to assist ourselves and others to embrace and resolve duality through living love. This act requires our realism, awareness, commitment, and access to our center.

In the geometric, multi-dimensional space of our body there are key nexus points that readily provide access to our psycho-spiritual resources. Access is essential for our success in using noetic psychology. Access aligns us with our innate self. The self of knowing that bridges through eternity and unites us with our multidimensional resources. We have loosened our identity from the self made mirrors that evolved through dualism and body centered identity. In this final section, we open and anchor channels of life and energy that are timeless wisdom. They are the timeless self. As our intimacy with the true self deepens, it dissolves the underlying distortion that create the pre-disposition for psychological imbalance.

**First Access.** The first access is through the resolution of limiting beliefs that block and imbalance our energy field, and becoming consciously connected to the energy movement within our physical body and our personal space. In the body we call this awareness a "felt sense." Around the body, I call it "energy-awareness," or *spatial seeing*. We "see" as experience. This access is covered in Chapter Six. We can now provide greater emphasis through perceptive activation of the geometric space and the matrix in which these processes occur. Again, this is review, with and emphasis on nexus through perception.

Begin as a journey moving your focus into your loving while moving your awareness into your physical body. Gently reveal to your awareness the tissues, bones, organs and cells of your body. Be aware of your felt-sense while you do this. Take note of the bi-lateral symmetry of your body. See your physical body filled with light as a means of amplifying this process. Remember the principle that life meets you at the level of your understanding and awareness. This is reality. This activity may reveal hidden or sleeping trauma and the associated judgments and beliefs. Forgive yourself for any judgments or limiting beliefs that arise in this process.

**Second Access.** Now extend your awareness along all surfaces of your skin, and then move your awareness into the space around your body, filling that space to include a sphere, or egg-shape, that extends an arms length dimension around your body. Identify with this space. It is within this personal space that all psychological dynamics, in the conventional sense, have their location. This is the location of the personal unconscious. The archetypal level is no longer abstract, it is in the space

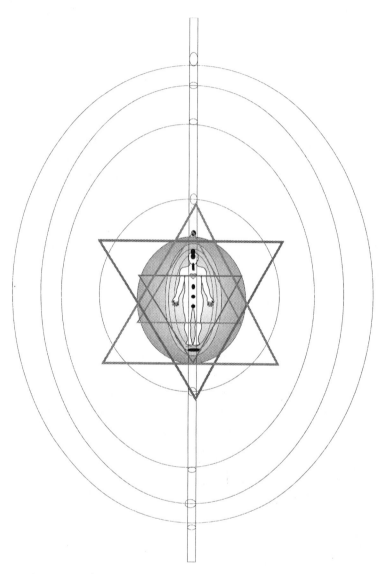

around and in your body. Being present in your space is the second nexus. It is the power of now. Again, forgive yourself for any self judgments or limiting beliefs that you become aware of.

**Third Access.** We now move to the transcendental access of transpersonal psychology. This is the self that transcends the ego and links with the universe. We find this nexus by directing our perception into a center-line that extends through the geometric center of our spherical space and physical body from the top of our head through our tail bone. Expand this center line to become a tube, at least the size of a fisted hand. Accomplish the expansion by looking at it as if it is so. This is perception through imagination. It is using your imagination as a lens. You look through your imagination-eyes at what is present. Once perceived, travel into this tube as your self. It is you as your sense of self. With this skill, Self is *locatable* to any dimension. You can focus by aligning that sense of identity that is you as an alignment within the tube, or see an image of a little you inside the tube. You are located where you organize your perception to be. This is a locus of intention. This is you as essence using intension as a sense organ. When all else dissolves, your awareness of location is you. When you are aware in a void, you are there. You are not the void. You are your sense of self. Ego cannot tolerate the void. If you thought you were the void, you would become afraid of annihilation, because the thought is in the mind, not the void. You can be universally aware of yourself as everything, yet this no-self-self is your awareness of self. You can be one with the void and you will experience peace. This is a key to self as essence.

Now, place your sense self in the tube. Establish this alignment by looking up and down in the tube and see what you see. Sensation is a form of seeing. Since you remain aware in your body and in your space, and, also, in the tube of light, you can say you have bi-located. You are aware in your physical body, your space, and in your center as your sense of self, or soul. In order to consolidate this access, breathe a golden light into the top and bottom of the tube, condensing it in your heart. On the out breath, breathe the light into your body and into your space.

Before we go further, simultaneously hold your attention in your center, your physical body and your space, while relaxing everything. As we add further access, we will also retain awareness in each preceding access. It is like each geometric location is a *locatable* self and is discretely aware and simultaneously aware as a unity.

**Fourth Access.** From your vantage point in the center of your head, expand the light in your head into a sphere of light about the size of your head. See yourself walking inside of that sphere of light. Move your senses into that image, feeling your buoyancy as you engage this space. As you continue, see yourself waking in nature. Be aware of your feet walking on the earth. Look down at your feet. What are you wearing? Be aware of the sights and sounds: the earth, vegetation, trees, flowers, birds, insects, breeze, etc. What are the sensations and fragrances?

Breathe nature through your body. Look up at the sky. Is it blue sky, clouds, or a night sky filled with stars? Look into the depths of the sky. Breathe in the sky. This journey takes you into the outer heart. Experience the love through Earth and Sky.

**Fifth Access.** Surrounded by the abundance of your heart-space, look into your physical heart. Within the domain of the actual physical heart is a hidden entrance to your sacred heart. Because of trauma and heart-break, we are often cautious of entering our sacred heart. In fact, we may have had so much injury that we have forgotten about the dynamo of loving power within us. It is a source of love that is beyond duality and, when in force, discontinues adversity. However, we have set the stage and are currently residing in the dynamic geometries of our activated self. At least, as far as we have gone. Feelings and images may arise of betrayal, disappointment or times when you tried to share your loving and could not. Forgive yourself for any self-judgment, limiting beliefs, or beliefs that you are a victim, or permanently damaged.

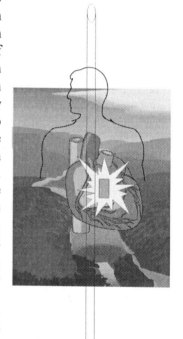

See your physical heart, and travel inside. Once inside, ask to be taken into your sacred heart and go with the guidance. You may have a sense of movement, see a small door, or just find yourself there. Once in this space, take in the sights and sounds, becoming oriented to your sacred heart. What do you see, hear, smell. If it is dark you can ask for light, to see, to be shown. This is the space in you that is the "sacred heart of Jesus," or the Sufi "Abode." It is the heart of Hanaman shown in Hinduism. It is here that you meet your inner beloved. Let the atmosphere of this place consume you. You are in the expansive realm within you of the sacred heart. Take your time. When you focus into the outer world of your life on earth, keep your awareness awake within this space. Be in the world, but not of it.

156

**Sixth Access.** Now, go to the location in your sacred heart where the golden column of light of your center axis passes through your sacred heart space. Ask for help if you are having trouble finding it. You can not make this happen. You just do it. Your intention will make it so and you will notice more as you practice over time. While in your sacred heart, stand in the column of light. You may experience it as a vortex of light. This vortex may have a clockwise spin when coming down from above your head, and a counter-clockwise spin when coming from beneath your feet. Explore whatever experience this nexus presents. Experience the extension of the light through your body, through the geometry of your spherical axis, and beyond your space below you. What do you sense, or see? Above you? What do you sense, or see? Enjoy.

**Seventh Access.** Travel up the tube, or vortex, out through the top of your physical head. Continue to about a hand length (six inches) above your head. You will come to a notable space, or place. This is the abode of the high-self. Some people say this is your soul. Certainly, it is a soul-contact. It is a spiritual guide that is a higher aspect of your personality. As you sense this energy, say: "show me yourself in a form I can relate to and understand." Say this with intention, love, and anticipation. The form in which it appears may change through continued familiarity. It will appear as a color, symbol, personification, feeling, or sensation. You might hear a sound or a voice. Engage this energy and establish a dialogue. Dialogue takes many forms from audible words, images, or a vague sense of some kind of exchange. You begin where you begin. When you activate this nexus, it activates the entire orb around and through your body that is the frequency of the high-self. The high-self will help you practice, so that you can easily repeat this process at each higher level of access. The felt-sense in your body strengthens the high-self connection through the basic-self. As you continue this practice and further exploration, your clarity and center become stronger. By activating the orb of each nexus, the higher energy pushes up through the unconscious, healing and surfacing patterns lodged in the depth of your unconscious.

**Eighth Access.** Continue up the column to at least 36 inches. Again, you will sense this location in response to your intention. This is the abode of the Divine Self, or I Am Self. Some people call this your "over soul." It is like an ombudsman in that it knows what to do and where to go for whatever is needed. It is comfortable in your multidimensional

157

self and reality. The protocol is the same. You ask that it appear in a form that you can relate to and understand and go on from there.

This access is on a "as-you-are-ready" basis. As a further empowerment, once you have merged with the divine self, say: Divine Self activate in every cell, matric, template, and code of my physical body, and observe while that process completes itself. Witness, or observation, appear to be necessary in the way perception functions in the creation of reality. This access demonstrates that you are truly divine.

**Ninth Access.** As you continue deeper up the light channel, you will encounter another presence. The frequency of your I Am is the entry into the temple of your Master Teacher. In truth it is a higher form of yourself as teacher of your selves. At this level, you encounter your self beyond time or place. Past and future is a deeper dimension of the present. Follow the previous protocol for engaging and activating the orb associated with this space. This access introduces your senses into an awareness of being cosmic in stature. You are able to access ancient wisdom and cosmic consciousness.

**Tenth Access.** As you continue deeper up the light channel, you will encounter another presence. This access is the Christ or Christos. It is the template for all that you are and will be. At this level you are encountering an aspect of your nature that is beyond any recent sense of yourself. This is the first taste of fulfilling our Divine destiny in the deepest sense. With this resource you can access the ability and authority to overcome all things. Use the previous protocol to engage, activate and anchor this consciousness. As you observe the action of this access, stay with it for awhile and see where it takes you or what it brings to you.

**Eleventh Access.** Continue up the vortex, channel, of light to approximately 67 feet above your head. This is the nexus of the Father/Mother God, the universal one. It is the first contact beyond your personal dimensions, taking you into the universal field of unconditional loving directly in contrast to filtering them through your own dimensional structure. This is the frequency of your source as a soul, the primal nature of how you strive to actualize your holiness through life experience. We have authority on this level to activate and balance our morphogenic field. We engage our authority in our DNA, resolve past life karma, and dissolve limiting core beliefs, and manifest new patterns directly. As we use the protocol to engage and activate this relationship, we are on the true level of our partnership with God. We do all things in partnership. We do our 10 % and God does its 90%. At this level, we have direct access to unconditional love. (www.thetahealing.com)

**Twelfth Access.** Soul Transcendence is the practice of traveling the sound current in your soul body into the a priori realm, which practically is an unlimited source of unconditional love. I introduce people to this approach through a simple spiritual exercise composed of chanting and a sound current meditation. This approach has many beneficial spiritual and psychological ramifications.

Chanting is a universal spiritual practice that creates an energy field, or context, and a relationship following the intention of the participants. Native American chants and Gregorian chants are examples of our natural understanding that sound forms a nexus with higher consciousness. In both cases, the focus is devotional, and the rhythms and patterns balance the mind and emotion of the participants and align them with the "Great" or "Holy" Spirit.

We are aware of the effect that music has on our moods. There are spiritual as well as physiological reasons for this. Science and religion have cosmologies that speak of the primordial role of sound in creation. The "big bang" and "in the beginning was the word" imply the seminal role of sound in creation. In the Saurat Shabd Yoga traditions of the mystery teaching, creation unfolds through sound and we return to our spiritual origins through the sound current. We are familiar with inspirational devotional music and its lifting influence. In Shabd Yoga, the adherents chant sanskrit names of God as a spiritual practice. This practice attunes our constitution to the energy of the sacred sounds, attracts the frequency of the sound current to us, and forms a nexus with it. Specific to this discussion, I use chanting with the group in a particular way.

I like to begin my classes with chanting Ani-Hu. Ani-Hu is a sanskrit phase meaning "cooperation with God." It promotes the energy of empathy. Sanskrit is an ancient language of archetypal sound. The characters were formed out of what the originators perceived as the forms made by the sounds. The "names of God," and there are many, attune the practitioner to the transcendental source of energy represented in the name used. Chanting Ani-Hu is similar to chanting "I love you." Love is the consciousness of Divine cooperation. In this case, it can be our inner child chanting to our higher self, our soul chanting to the All Parent, or the holiness within us chanting to the holiness within each of us. In some traditions, Ani-Hu means "I Am." So, the vibration is "I am love," "we are love," or "Love is." Chants such as 'Allah Hoo' (Sufi) resonate to a "God-level," in a similar way to the phrase "hallelujah" (Christian). The spiritual exercise follows a protocol, or sequence as follows:

1.  As we chant together we generate a harmonizing, healing and balancing energy that shapes the context we share into a *Holy presence on holy ground.*

2.  As our chanting gains momentum, images and circumstances that are unresolved arise in our individual awareness. Since we are already chanting, we meet the awareness of the unresolved pattern with "cooperation with God" or "I love you." This has a resolving and balancing influence.

3.  As we chant, each person's balance is enhanced and contributes to raising the frequency of the group. In turn, the group, and in-flowing spiritual energy, influence greater healing and balance for individuals in the group.

4.  At some point (at least 30 minutes, if it is convenient), we transition from chanting out loud to inner chanting with the *voice* of our mind and heart. With this transition, we focus in, up, and out through the crown chakra. This action promotes a nexus between our holiness and the sound current, which is an audible life stream of the original holiness that is the source of all. In the lineage of "soul-transcendence," we embark on a journey to our spiritual home.

5.  We alternately chant and listen, going with the flow of the energy. This flow may draw us upward to higher realms or be in-filling and healing, or both. This pull to higher consciousness is very different from the dissociation of psychological projection, it is the unification of all of the dimensions with source. This inner practice may require a strong focus of our will into the sound-stream while the business of the mind pass by us, as if we were in a boat on a river of sound watching the mind on the shore. We may at first hear the sound as a silence.

6.    Finally, we surrender to the invitation that responds to our chanting, and give ourselves permission to abide with that field of experience, or reality, for awhile. Listen and be heard.

7.    After some period of time, we open our eyes and center into our physical bodies. This enfolds heaven and earth together and aligns us from the physical through the soul levels.

This activity creates a unified field: a *sacred ground,* as it applies to our relationship to the earth, and as it applies to the *sacred ground* of the transcendent worlds. The above practice is how I guide the process in my groups. As a personal practice, you may decide to chant out loud for a shorter time, or not at all. You may prefer to move to the inner experience directly. As a personal meditation practice, it is very powerful and may require a time of building the energy for deeper experience. It will have a profound effect on your access. If you are drawn to this form of meditation, you may want to go beyond this discussion. For years, I have studied with a teacher that offers guidance in this way. It is a deep and ancient teaching of the *sound current* and goes far beyond this writing. If your are interested, go to www.msia.org. Otherwise, continue practicing the possibilities offered in this writing and go where it leads you. Test everything.

## APPLIED SPIRITUAL PSYCHOLOGY

Now that we have access, an introduction to the geometry of self, awareness of life energy, the nature of perception, phenomenological discovery, and noetic therapy, we are ready for a further step in understanding the dynamic in the fabric of self. We are self perpetuating. The good news is that we are eternal. The bad news is that whatever or whomever we have decided that we are, we will perpetuate that self and the environment that supports it.

When we activate our awareness of self in our soul-axis, individuation takes a dramatic turn. Before we became aware of our greater self through access, our transformation was limited to tracking and transforming beliefs as the end-all-and-be-all of the therapeutic process. Now we are capable of having a personal experience with our higher aspects and with eternity itself. We experience our holiness in our body through the access of our center. When we align in, and identify with, the infinite energy of our center, firmly anchored in the earth and source, a vortex activates that illuminates and draws to it the miasmas of the personal and collective unconscious. By holding our center as a witness and imagining life as the "face of Eternity," the miasmas, or forms of distorted creativity, dissolve. There is an old saying that "if you look upon the face of God you will die." As a metaphor, "look upon the face of God and your false self will die." A new clarity appears in the inner and outer mirror of life. Before, we could see the metaphor of life as it reflected our unconscious back to us through daily living. Now, we see a light behind the mirror as if we were meeting our selves coming to us through our life experience, from the horizon or our perception. A light radiates from within that reflects on the mirror and another light that radiates through the mirror from the universal levels of the unconscious. We see this light visually, as sensations, movements, textures, or as images and as sound.

In the following diagram, we can visualize the dynamic action of perception. Perception is a confluence of our personal psychology, genetic make up, and the metaphysical and spiritual geometries.

Continuing with our exploration of the unconscious mind, as the space in which our physical body is nested, we can form a picture of how levels of personal, cultural, and natural history form levels of perception that limit and distort our experience. Common sense tells us there is a deeper implicate order from which an undistorted template of self once emerged. This template is the source of our motivation to fulfill our true nature through the challenges of our lives. Close at hand are the personal beliefs that we formed from our responses to the situations and circumstances of our lives. Of concern are the beliefs that limit and distort the picture of our self from the truth or essence of who we are. From a Buddhist sense, this self is a no-self, and that is compatible with this discussion, because the ego, based on duality, dissolves into a non-dual experience, which we experience as everything and self. The coding for truth or essence can be accessed through our center or soul axis. When we wake-up in the center, we can access the flow of energy that carries these codes. We become able to inform our selves inwardly of our true nature. This occurs beyond "our truth" as truth itself. The central flow of energy also enables us to resolve distortions by bringing the higher information, as energy, into the lower.

The double arrows show the projection/reflection of each moment, or breath cycle. Limiting and distorted beliefs pull our awareness away from our center. Our personal psychology exists as if we had no center in the form of a central axis composed of dynamic, living source energy. Our physical body is the recipient of our self

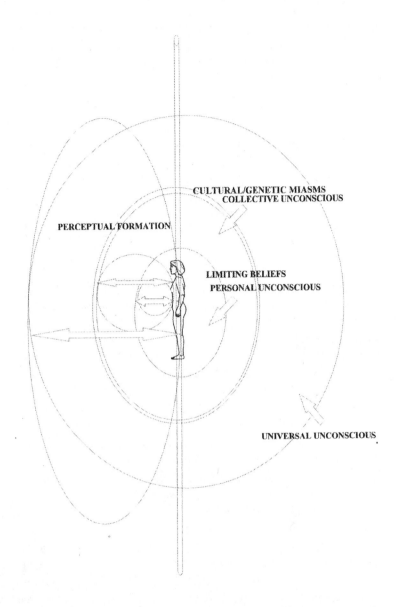

CULTURAL/GENETIC MIASMS
COLLECTIVE UNCONSCIOUS

PERCEPTUAL FORMATION

LIMITING BELIEFS
PERSONAL UNCONSCIOUS

UNIVERSAL UNCONSCIOUS

concept. The center exist, but for all practical purposes, it exists abstractly. The reinforcement cycle of perception bases reality on our physical body. Consequently, we perceive our body and our space as our total reality.

Beneath the frequency of our own created beliefs are the underlying influence of the collective unconscious. Each of the fields encompasses and interpenetrates the field below it. In like manner our

163

perception is sustained through the projection/reflection cycle. The thought forms of the collective cause a predisposition to think, choose and act in certain ways. Classic phrases from the collective are:

> You know your worth through comparison to others.
> You are innately bad or unworthy.
> When you do good you are good.
> When you do bad you are bad.
> Women find their value through men.
> To be safe we have to control resources and dominate others.
> Redemption is external.
> Men find their value through rescuing women.
> Consciousness emerges from physical evolution.
> Etcetera.

A list like this can go on and on. As individuals, we can list the phrases that underlie and are foundational to our approach to life. These patterns are ancient and permeate our human existence whether or not we participated in their creation or not. These beliefs often dissolve when we are actively centered and bring them into our awareness. In order to dissolve personal beliefs, we must incorporate some form of self-forgiveness or epiphany that reveals our divine self in relationship to the thought forms created by limiting beliefs.

As we resolve the miasmas of the personal and collective unconscious, our conscious self expands beyond the duality of these levels. As the experience of a non-dual unity of these various forces of life emerges, the barrier between the distortions of the collective and personal levels dissolves and the original pattern of human health merges within all of our levels and expressions and we spontaneously and progressively correct ourselves.

Rudolf Steiner observed that the our soul approaches from the horizon. When our perception is limited to the personal and collective unconscious, reality reinforces our beliefs as true. As we expand beyond this limitation in our noetic field, our reality field dissolves the patterns and codes that produce distortion. We see truth directly. As Paul said: "I look through a glass darkly, yet face to face."

Conventional psychology effectively explores our issues and needs through finding and correcting beliefs and trauma produced developmentally along our time line. This is an effective therapeutic approach. It becomes more effective as we experientially identify with our center and expand that light to encompass our body, mind and emotions. As we increasingly identify with center and reach up and affiliate our sense of self with higher archetypal and spiritual levels of self, we reverse the trends of our negative, reversed creations. By that, I mean that as we stand in the noegenesis of our truth and light, and identify with it, our shadow is pulled into the light. Searching the dark corners of our developmental traumas becomes much easier when the traumas and their constellated beliefs are pulled into the light.

The force propelling this process is our core impetus to actualize. All of our creations and adopted creations seek actualization. Because of that, we either fulfill them through completing the consequence of that choice or pulling our essence out of the distortion, thereby restoring our self to our self. This is the "It of Itself." When we find ourselves in the non-dual experience of universal love, we declare in that moment: "This I am." Individuation is complete, and the boundary of our separated self dissolves.

The practice of spiritual psychology requires the facilitator to be able to move to a heightened state. Preparation is continual. The practitioner is evolving a self based on a center of universal intelligence, contained in the encompassing field of universal love. To do this, we reach into our center and out to the universal field. As we do this, an inductive response occurs in our client that stirs a remembrance of essence. In this way all therapeutic forms are enhanced by the perceptual state of the practitioner. The shadow of the client is called forward into the light.

## Fabric of Self

The *fabric of self* is woven through the co-creative intimacy of life. As we become increasingly aware and connected with life, we choose consciously to harmonize that fabric with the universe and our origins. This choice is our destiny.

This book arouse out of courses that I teach in noetic field therapy and ancient mysteries applied to modern living, forty years of practicing, and teaching Noetic Field Balancing, and the experience of developing Southwestern College in Santa Fe, New Mexico, as a center for educating therapists. As we apply this to our own health and well being and the health and well being of others, we see a pattern of service. On the dimension of ego living on Earth, our lives deliver to us the experiences that enable the soul to actualize itself. This is the realm of therapeutic transformation. On the dimension of our internal frontiers, the territory of the soul, we journey inward into essence, into source. This journey activates our spiritual power. By so doing, we open inward doors to the realms of self and God. This has impact in the world. It pushes to the surface our unresolved issues and forgotten creation. The outer and inner challenges increase and intensify. As if one mirror was not enough. During this phase, it can be helpful to have a guide, or witness. As we increasingly trust our holiness, the stress subsides. It may only take a simple self forgiveness, on any level, dimension or embodiment, for each time that we have chosen away from the experience of our center, or soul. As the inner light intensifies, we often become calmer. Symptoms of center are joy, peace, love, enthusiasm, abundance, or liberation. Finally, we invite, or command (not demand) all of the shadows within us on any level or dimension to come forward into the light and dissolve.

This is our way. It is in the process of living on earth that we come to realize that this incarnation is a *foot print of eternity*.